SPANISH PLACES

A guide to walking in the Spanish mountains

LOS PICOS
DE EUROPA

BOOK ONE OF A SERIES

PHIL LAWLER

First Edition published 2018 by
Spanish Steps,
Skipton
North Yorkshire

Disclaimer
The author has taken all reasonable effort to ensure that the information
herein is accurate, however the author accepts no responsibility if it is
not, nor if unforeseen circumstances occur while doing the routes. We
would also advise that in planning your route you check local transport,
accommodation and please be aware that some paths and rights of
way may be affected by changes such as development or weather. We
would appreciate any information regarding changes. You can do this by
contacting the Publisher in the first instance.

Photographs and Maps © 2017 Phil Lawler

The author has his own website: http://www.spanishtrailsco.com

Production by 2QT Limited (Publishing), Settle, North Yorkshire
Cover design by Charlotte Mouncey (using authors photograph)

Printed in Great Britain by
TJ International UK Ltd

A CIP catalogue record for this book is available
from the British Library
ISBN - 978-0-9955797-0-5

The author on Pico Padierna – **WALK 18**

DISCLAIMER

The walk descriptions and maps in this publication are as accurate as I can make them, but things change and I cannot guarantee that everything is always up to date or 100 per cent correct. You must take all reasonable precautions and wear adequate clothing, carry waterproofs, a mobile phone and so on, just as you would when hill walking in the UK. You also need protection from the sun. And let somebody know where you are going when you set out.

All users of this information do so entirely at their own risk.

ABOUT THE AUTHOR

Phil Lawler spent his formative years walking the Yorkshire Dales. In later years his job took him to live in Madrid. He worked in most of Spain's larger cities, and he got to know the country and its mountains intimately. In the process he got to understand Spanish culture and gained a fluent command of the language.

After leaving his 'proper' job in Madrid, Phil spent several years leading walking groups in different parts of the country. Now retired, he still walks in Spain, principally in the Picos de Europa, the Sierra de Guadarrama, Cazorla and the Sierra Almijara, but also in the Pyrenees, Somiedo and other parts.

In the natural park of the Sierra Tejeda and Almijara there is nowadays a network of footpaths. But back in the 1990s they scarcely existed. Phil and friends spent time exploring and clearing the old mule trails there, which had been out of use for many years. There were no maps of these routes, and even now, although mapping has improved, many of the best paths are not shown.

You are welcome to visit www.spanishtrailsco.com or to contact Phil on info@spanishtrailsco.com if you enjoy what he has written here and need more information.

Contents

DISCLAIMER 3

ABOUT THE AUTHOR 4

LOS PICOS DE EUROPA 9

AREA MAP 14

THE WALKS IN ORDER OF DIFFICULTY 15

HILL WALKS IN THE PICOS DE EUROPA 17

WALK NO. 1
ALEVIA TO PICO PAISANO 23

WALK NO. 2
URDÓN TO TRESVISO 27

WALK NO. 3
OCEÑO TO THE PEAK OF VIGUERAS 30

WALK NO. 4
CÁRAVES TO ARENAS DE CABRALES 35

WALK NO. 5
SOTRES TO PICA FUENTE SOLES (1,564m) 39

WALK NO. 6
ESCARANDI TO THE PEAK OF CUETU TEJAU (2,129m) 42

WALK NO. 7
CIRCUIT FROM SOTRES VIA TIELVE 46

WALK NO. 8
SOTRES TO PEÑA MAIN AND TIELVE 49

WALK NO. 9
THREE PEAKS OF LA JUNCIANA, SAGRADO CORAZÓN AND
SAMELAR 54

WALK NO. 10
ESCARANDI TO LA RASA DEL INAGOTABLE (2,282m) AND
GRAJAL DE ABAJO (2,246m) 59

WALK NO. 11
JITO DE ESCARANDI TO SILLA DEL CABALLO CIMERO (2,436m)......62

WALK NO. 12
VEGA DE URRIELLO, HORCADOS ROJOS AND ALIVA.....................67

WALK NO. 13
INVERNALES DEL TEXU TO THE PEAK OF PEÑA CASTIL (2,444m)....72

WALK NO. 14
SOTRES TO THE ALIVA REFUGE AND THE FUENTE DÉ CABLE CAR...76

WALK NO. 15
SOTRES TO TRESVISO..80

WALK NO. 16
THE VALDOMINGUERO RIDGE...84

WALK NO. 17
FUENTE DÉ CABLE CAR TO TORRE DE HORCADOS ROJOS...............88

WALK NO. 18
FUENTE DÉ TO VEGA DE LLORDES..93

WALK NO. 19
ALIVA REFUGE TO THE PICOS DE CÁMARA.................................98

WALK NO. 20
CORISCAO..101

WALK NO. 21
POSADA DE VALDEÓN TO CORONA CIRCUIT..............................104

WALK NO. 22
POSADA DE VALDEÓN TO THE PEAK OF LOS MOLEDIZOS...............108

WALK NO. 23
POSADA DE VALDEÓN TO THE PEAK OF TORRE BERMEJA...............112

WALK NO. 24
CORDIÑANES TO THE COLLADO JERMOSO REFUGE.....................116

WALK NO. 25
PEÑA REMOÑA PEAK..120

WALK NO. 26
CAIN TO PONCEBOS THROUGH THE CARES GORGE 127

WALK NO. 27
CAIN TO THE ARIO REFUGE VIA THE SEDOS DE OLISEDA 133

WALK NO. 28
VEGA DE ARIO TO CAIN VIA THE CULIEMBRO GULLY 138

WALK NO. 29
PANDERRUEDAS TO THE PEAK OF JARIO 141

WALK NO. 30
PANDERRUEDAS TO THE PEAK OF GILDAR (2,078m) 146

WALK NO. 31
TORRE DEL FRIERO AND THE CANAL DE ASOTIN 150

WALK 32
LAGO DE LA ERCINA TO CAIN VIA THE ARIO REFUGE 155

WALK NO. 33
LA REDONDIELLA CIRCUIT FROM LAGO DE LA ERCINA 160

WALK NO. 34
MIRADOR DE ORDIALES AND PICO COTALBA 164

Balcon de Pilatos - **WALK 2**

LOS PICOS DE EUROPA

AN INTRODUCTION

The Picos de Europa are the highest peaks of the Cantabrian Mountains (the Cordillera Cantábrica), a mountain range running parallel with the Spanish Atlantic coastline in the far north of the country. The National Park of the Picos covers a small area, only about 50 kilometres by 25, but within those boundaries there is a vast choice of great walks. Although the northern slopes are within just a few kilometres of the sea, the hills rise to a height of 2,650 metres, with jagged limestone peaks separated by green valleys and rivers. The highlights are the Cares Gorge, the Covadonga lakes and the remarkable rock tower of Picu Urriellu (also called the Naranjo de Bulnes).

The Picos are west of Santander and east of Oviedo. The walking can best be accessed from the villages of Sotres in the north-east and from Posada de Valdeón in the south-west. These villages give direct access on foot to some of the highest peaks. More popular with tourists are Potes in the south-east, Arenas de Cabrales to the north and Cangas de Onis to the north-west. These towns offer ample accommodation, but require transport to get you to the main walking areas. A particular favourite with tourists is Fuente Dé, 23 km from Potes, where a cable car rises 600 metres up a cliff face to reach high-level walking with no effort, apart from the strain on your wallet.

Walking in the central Picos is generally moderate to strenuous. Some of the highest peaks can only be reached by sleeping at mountain refuges – where you can get a good meal, but sleep in dormitories. If you prefer creature comforts, there is good walking from Sotres and Posada de Valdeón, where comfortable accommodation is available.

The Picos are a serious mountain range, and therefore inherently involve some danger. Some walks can involve exposure, and require a good head for heights. In my walk descriptions I indicate where this applies. Except where indicated, the walks in this collection do not involve serious exposure, but care must always be taken. There is not a lot of really easy walking in the Picos, and in any case this guide is for hill walkers. However, I have included some easier routes, as indicated in the summary of the walks.

TRAVEL

From the UK, at the time of writing, there are flights from Stansted to Bilbao, Santander and Asturias, and from Manchester to Bilbao. Once you arrive in Spain, the easiest thing is to hire a car, although one way to travel if you have plenty of time is on the FEVE narrow guage railway, which runs along the north coast. The Picos can then be accessed by bus from the station at Arriondas to the west and at Unquera to the east.

Bus services run along the coast, connecting Bilbao, Santander and Oviedo with smaller towns on the periphery of the Picos. Local bus services within the national park are rare (there are hardly any roads, never mind buses), but taxis are plentiful and include four-wheel drives.

You can walk through the Picos from north to south in a distance of about 20 kilometres, but to drive it can be up to 120 km because the bendy roads go right round the perimeter of the national park.

RECOMMENDED MAPS

Adrados Ediciones publish 1:25,000 maps, one for the Central and the Eastern massifs (ISBN: 978-84-933177-8-2), and one for the Western massif (ISBN: 978-84-933177-9-9). By comparison with most Spanish maps these are excellent, and they show many footpaths. However, many paths are not shown. To follow my routes you should use these Adrados maps in conjunction with my sketch maps, which may look crude but tell you what you need to know.

For a view of the wider area, there is also an Adrados map at 1:50,000 scale (ISBN: 978-84-933177-7-5).

GPS

GPS technology and maps are constantly changing, so I cannot claim to know the best answer for GPS mapping in the Picos. The Alpina 25,000 map seems to have recently been discontinued. There are alternatives but you will need to do your own research.

At the end of each walk description I have provided some relevant GPS waypoint references, which are stated in accordance with the Spanish grid UTM and Datum WGS84.

Some words of warning:

- In some of the valleys of the Picos, GPS signals are erratic or non-existent.

- The paper maps and the GPS maps show footpaths in their approximate position. At times you may find yourself walking some distance away from the path shown on the GPS map.

- At the end of each walk description I give a few key GPS references. These are approximate. You must not treat them as exact references. The referencing and the mapping are difficult, due to the complexity of the terrain. You must treat my GPS references as a general guide only.

- In Spain, the presence of a path on a map does not guarantee that it actually exists. It may have been there years ago. Similarly, there are good paths now in existence which are not shown on any published maps. So a 100 per cent reliance on a GPS for navigation is not recommended.

TERMINOLOGY

Some editions of the recommended maps are written in Spanish, while others use the local Asturian language. As an example, the central peak known in Spanish as Pico Urriello is known in Asturian as Picu Urrlellu.

Also, the terminology can vary between different parts of the Picos. The national park sits partly in the province of León, partly in Asturias, and partly in Cantabria, each of which has its own terminology.

A few significant translations follow:

Spanish or Asturian	English
Canal	Gully
Horcada	Col (a gap between two hills)
Collado or collada	Col (a gap between two hills)
Mirador	Viewpoint
Pico	Peak
Torre	Peak
Garganta	Gorge
Rio	River or stream
Peña	Hill
Fuente	Spring (often with a tap. Untreated water.)
Vega	Meadow

GENERAL ADVICE

Since this book is written for experienced hill walkers, I will not provide a detailed list of gear. Just bear in mind that this is the north of Spain, not the Mediterranean, and the weather can be as variable as in the UK. You will need all the gear that you would take if you were walking in the UK, plus sun protection. Layers of light clothing are preferable to heavy clothes.

There are huge differences between the seasons. From December to June there can be deep snow, even at modest altitudes. July and August can be very warm. The best times for walking at high levels tend to be from late August through to October, when temperatures are warm, and when nights are not normally freezing. Before late June the snow can be an obstacle at high level. Snowshoeing would perhaps be an alternative, but I am not experienced in that activity.

THE WALKS

The walks are organised in a geographical sequence, beginning in the north-east and going around the Picos in a clockwise direction. I also list the walks in their order of difficulty. And in the walk summaries I give an idea of the degree of exposure.

Assessments of difficulty and of exposure are essentially subjective. A difficult walk for one person can be an easy one for another. If you try one of my walks it will help you to judge the remainder.

Each walk has directions, along with a sketch map, which you should use to accompany whichever topographical map you use. The sketch maps are not to exact scale. But they are, generally speaking, drawn from my own GPS tracks.

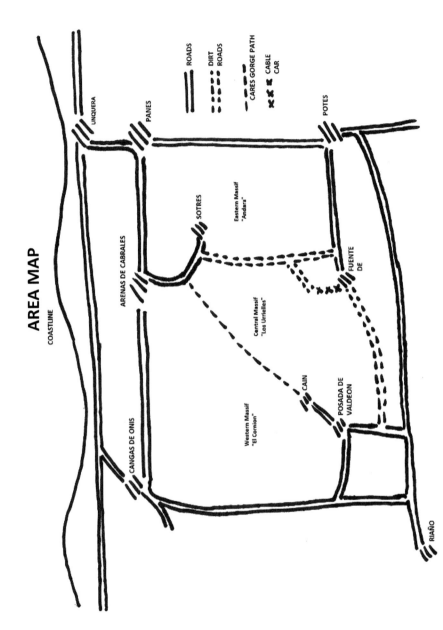

THE WALKS IN ORDER OF DIFFICULTY

In the main index the walks are numbered in a geographical sequence, beginning in the north-eastern corner of the Picos and then roughly in clockwise order.

The main index shows the approximate distances involved, along with an estimate of the total ascent in metres and the degree of difficulty and exposure. The latter are subjective. You should attempt one of my easier walks to get an idea of the way I assess these, before embarking on any of the more difficult routes.

The following index shows the walks in the order of difficulty which I have given to them:

Walk 33	La Redondiella	Easy
Walk 5	Sotres to Pica Fuente Soles	Easy
Walk 14	Sotres to Aliva and Fuente De	Easy
Walk 20	Coriscao	Easy
Walk 1	Alevia to Pico Paisano	Easy
Walk 15	Escarandi to Tresviso	Easy
Walk 7	Sotres to Tielve	Easy or moderate
Walk 21	Posada de Valdeon to Corona	Easy or moderate
Walk 26	Cares Gorge	Easy with a more strenuous option
Walk 29	Panderruedas to Jario peak	Easy with strenuous options
Walk 19	Aliva to Picos de Camara	Moderate
Walk 4	Caraves to Arenas	Moderate
Walk 10	Escarandi to La Rasa	Moderate

Walk 2	Urdon to Tresviso	Moderate
Walk 3	Oceño to Vigueras	Moderate
Walk 28	Ario to Cain via Culiembro	Moderate
Walk 30	Panderruedas to Gildar	Moderate (with an exposed option)
Walk 17	Torre de Horcados Rojos	Moderate or Strenuous
Walk 34	Mirador de Ordiales and Pico Cotalba	Moderate or Strenuous
Walk 8	Sotres to Pena Main and Tielve	Strenuous
Walk 9	Escarandi to Sagrado Corazon	Strenuous
Walk 6	Escarandi to Cuetu Tejayu	Strenuous
Walk 13	Texu to Pena Castil peak	Strenuous
Walk 18	Fuente De to Vega de Llordes	Strenuous
Walk 22	Posada de Valdeon to Los Moledizos	Strenuous
Walk 23	Posada de Valdeon to Torre Bermeja	Strenuous
Walk 24	Cordiñanes to Collado Jermoso	Strenuous
Walk 25	Pandetrave to Peña Remoña	Strenuous
Walk 32	Lago Ercina to Cain via Ario	Strenuous
Walk 12	Sotres to Urriellu and Aliva	Very strenuous
Walk 11	Silla del Caballo Cimero	Strenuous and exposed
Walk 16	Valdominguero	Strenuous and exposed
Walk 27	Cain to Ario via Sedos de Oliseda	Strenuous and exposed
Walk 31	Torre del Friero	Strenuous and exposed

HILL WALKS IN THE PICOS DE EUROPA

WALKS NEAR PANES:

WALK NO.	ROUTE	DISTANCE (kms)	ASCENT (metres)
PICOS 1 Easy	Alevia to Pico Paisano	14	735

Description: *Outlying Peak*

PICOS 2 Moderate	Urdon to Tresviso	6 each way	830

Description: *Big ascent to a remote village*

PICOS 3 Moderate	Oceño to Vigueras	7.5 each way	1,050

Description: *A minor but worthwhile peak*

PICOS 4 Moderate	Caraves to Arenas de Cabrales	10 linear	870

Description: *Traverse high above the Cares river*

WALKS NEAR SOTRES:

WALK NO,	ROUTE	DISTANCE (kms)	ASCENT (metres)
PICOS 5 Easy	Sotres to Pica Fuente Soles	3 each way	560

Description: *Local smaller peak*

PICOS 6 Strenuous	Escarandi to Cuetu Tejau	14	1,100

Description: *High peak overlooking Sotres*

PICOS 7 Moderate	Sotres to Tielve	13	900

Description: *Mid-level circuit. Good views*

PICOS 8 Moderate	Sotres to Peña Main and Tielve	11	800

Description: *A modest peak with great views*

PICOS 9 Strenuous or moderate	La Junciana, Sagrado Corazon and Samelar	17	1,350

Description: *Three accessible peaks*

PICOS 10 Moderate	Escarandi to La Rasa and Grajal de Abajo	15	1,150

Description: *Two peaks*

PICOS 11 Strenuous	Sotres to Silla del Caballo Cimero	18	1,350

Description: *Exposed ridge scramble*

PICOS 12 Very strenuous	Sotres to the Vega de Urriellu and Aliva	22	1,900

Description: *The heart of the Picos*

PICOS 13 Strenuous	Texu to Pena Castil	16	1,650

Description: *A big ascent to a high peak*

PICOS 14 Easy	Sotres to Aliva and Fuente De	13	1,100

Description: *Traverse*

PICOS 15 Easy	Escarandi to Tresviso	9 each way	250 out, 650 back

Description: *Village to village*

PICOS 16 Strenuous	Valdominguero	15	1,150

Description: *Exposed ridge scramble*

WALKS NEAR FUENTE DE:

WALK NO,	ROUTE	DISTANCE (kms)	ASCENT (metres)
PICOS 17 Moderate	Cable car to Horcados Rojos	11	1,070

Description: *A peak near the cable car (with access to other peaks)*

PICOS 18 Strenuous	Fuente De to Vega de Llordes (2 optional routes)	11 or 13	1,070

Description: *High Level Traverse. A little exposure on the cable car route*

PICOS 19 Moderate	Aliva to Picos de Camara	6 each way	630

Description: *A relatively easy high peak*

PICOS 20 Easy	Ascent of Coriscao	6.5 each way	800

Description: *An outlying peak*

WALKS NEAR POSADA DE VALDEON:

WALK NO,	ROUTE	DISTANCE (kms)	ASCENT (metres)
PICOS 21 Easy or moderate	Posada de Valdeon to Corona circuit	14	650

Description: *A circuit of the Valdeon valley*

PICOS 22 Strenuous	Posada de Valdeon to Los Moledizos	9 each way	1,440

Description: *High peak*

PICOS 23 Strenuous	Posada de Valdeon to Torre Bermeja	7 each way	1,500

Description: *High peak*

PICOS 24 Strenuous	Cordiñanes to Collado Jermoso	9 each way	1,400

Description: *Ascent to a mountain refuge*

PICOS 25 Strenuous	Pandetrave to Peña Remoña	9.5 each way	1,100

Description: *High peak*

PICOS 26 Easy with a more strenuous option	Cain to Poncebos through the Cares Gorge	22	400

Description: *Spectacular gorge*

PICOS 27 Strenuous	Cain to Ario via Sedos de Oliseda	10	1,500

Description: *Ascent to a mountain refuge, with an exposed scramble*

| PICOS 28 Moderate | Ario to Cain via the Culiembro gully | 14 | 275 (1,400 descent) |

Description: *Big descent from a refuge*

| PICOS 29 Easy with moderate options | Panderruedas to Jario | 12 | 600 |

Description: *Outlying peak*

| PICOS 30 Moderate | Panderruedas to Gildar | 14 | 890 |

Description: *Outlying peak*

| PICOS 31 Strenuous | Torre del Friero | 16 | 1,360 |

Description: *An exposed high peak*

WALKS NEAR COVADONGA:

WALK NO,	ROUTE	DISTANCE (kms)	ASCENT (metres)
PICOS 32 Strenuous	Lago Ercina to Cain via Ario refuge	17	750

Description: *High level traverse*

| PICOS 33 Easy | Lago Ercina to La Redondiella | 8 | 350 |

Description: *Easy circuit from the lakes*

| PICOS 34 Moderate | Lago de Enol to the Ordiales viewpoint, Cotalba peak and Vegarredonda refuge | 12 | 1,050 |

Description: *Moderate walking to a great viewpoint and a peak*

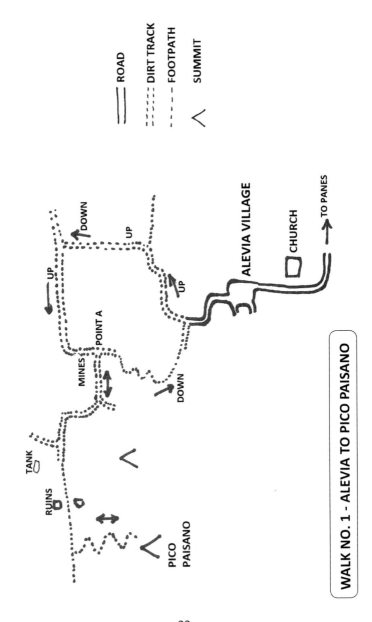

ROAD
DIRT TRACK
FOOTPATH
SUMMIT

DOWN
UP
UP
UP
UP
DOWN
POINT A
MINES
TANK
RUINS
PICO PAISANO
ALEVIA VILLAGE
CHURCH
TO PANES

WALK NO. 1 - ALEVIA TO PICO PAISANO

WALK NO. 1

ALEVIA TO PICO PAISANO

A lovely peak in the Sierra de Cuera, in the Picos foothills. Overlooking the coast, with great views into the central range.

Distance	14 kms
Ascent	735 metres
Overall grade	Easy
Terrain	Tracks, footpaths and grass
Exposure	Nil
Highest point	814 metres

- Start and finish at Alevia, a village high up a hill 2 km north of Panes. Begin the walk at the church. You can park next to it.

- Signposting in this area keeps changing. You may see signs leading you along this route, but in the opposite direction.

Walk round to the front of the church, for great views down to Panes and to the pointed peak of Peñamellera to the west. Go uphill through the village. Pass through a small square with a *bolera* (skittle alley) in the centre, and go straight on. Look for yellow and white paint marks showing the route. Go slightly left, near a water tap. Then the street swings right and uphill, and passes a water treatment plant on your left. The road becomes a concrete track and ascends very steeply to the north-east.

- The track soon swings left, and the gradient eases. You will see a radio antenna on a hill above. The track will take you below and to the right-hand side of this hill. Ignore a signpost for a footpath to the right. You will pass corrals for livestock, and you may well see cattle and goats. The track becomes dirt instead of concrete. Continue and the track eventually descends to reach another track coming uphill from the villages on the north side of the hills. Turn left uphill on this track. There are good views to the north, with the village of Boquerizo just below and the Atlantic coastline beyond. Ascend gradually to the west, to encounter some disused mines. Swing to the left (south) in front of the mines, on a grassy track. There is a watering hole used by cattle and horses. Beyond it, take a track to the right at a junction. You will return to this point on the return leg. **This is Point A on the sketch map.**

- Having turned right, the track now ascends gradually, going west once more and passing through grassy meadows that are rich with wild flowers in the spring. Avoid a track going to the left, and swing to the right and pass in front of an old mineshaft. The track swings left again. You will see another antenna on a hill, but our target is the next summit beyond it. The track reaches a junction with another track coming in from the right, with a watering tank for animals below. Turn left here. Continue in a westerly direction and pass by ruined farm buildings, and continue on to a meadow (Braña la Pipa) with explanatory signposts (these may have fallen down) and watering for animals. Pico Paisano is now ahead of you.

- Continue on a path past some ruins and keep to the right (northern) side of the peak. Halfway along its flanks simply turn left and ascend to the peak in zigzags. It is very steep, but there is no difficulty otherwise as the slopes are entirely grassy. The optimum route keeps over to the left. If you head more or less south-east as you ascend, you can turn right where you reach the ridgeline to reach the summit. The views from the peak are terrific.

- *At the summit you will find a little chapel – a monument to the Indianos, the people who migrated to the Americas in the sixteenth century. Their descendants returned many years later, bringing with them the lovely architecture that you will see in Alevia at the end of the walk. 'Paisano' means somebody from the same country. By the chapel there is a small monument to these people. The national Archivo de Indianos Foundation-Museum of Emigration is in nearby Colombres (but it is currently under threat due to economic reasons).*

- Descend from the peak by the way you came. At the first buildings you can go straight on, or you can turn right and follow the edge of the ridge to make a circuit back to Braña la Pipa. From there follow the outward route back to Point A, and turn right there. After 200 metres there is a fence, with the remnants of an old mining hoist. Turn sharp right here and go through a gate. A path goes downhill leading all the way back to Alevia. It is marked with paint, and most of it is easy to follow. It zigzags down a steep slope and then takes a more level route. At a fork, the correct path is the right fork – but it may not appear so. If you lose the path, go back and try again.

- The final stretch is on a track which is often muddy and may have overhanging brambles. At the end of the track turn right back into the village, and note the Indianos houses.

GPS REFERENCES (UTM)

Start and finish	370556 4799071
Junction	369893 4800949
Point A	369214 4800159
Summit	367181 4800308
Descent to village	369326 4799908

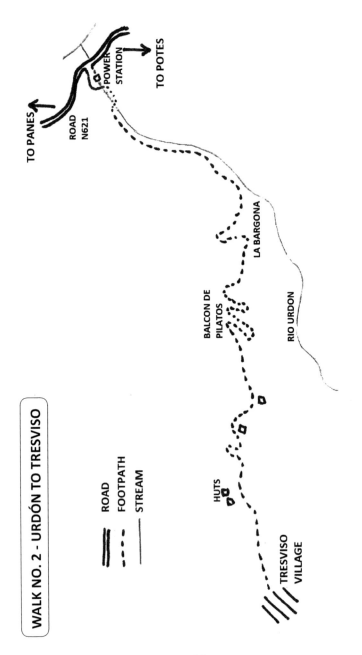

WALK NO. 2 - URDÓN TO TRESVISO

ROAD
FOOTPATH
STREAM

TO PANES

ROAD
N621

POWER
STATION

TO POTES

LA BARGONA

BALCON DE
PILATOS

RIO URDON

HUTS

TRESVISO
VILLAGE

WALK NO. 2

URDÓN TO TRESVISO

A popular ascent on a well-defined path from the Hermida gorge to the remote village of Tresviso. It is most unusual to make an ascent of over 800 metres and find a village at the top. This path is marked in yellow and white as the official route "PR-PNPE30".

Distance	12 km round trip
Ascent	830 metres
Overall grade	Moderate
Terrain	Stony, zigzag footpath
Exposure	Airy aspect, but no real exposure.
Highest point	900 metres

Tresviso is a village at 900 metres above sea level, accessible by road only from the west, via Arenas de Cabrales. The road is a dead end at Tresviso. The only approach from the east is by this unique footpath.

There are great views along the walk, but part of the attraction is the footpath itself. It is an old zinc mining track from the mid nineteenth century. The mines were abandoned long ago.

The spectacular path, when viewed from photos, appears considerably exposed. But in fact the signposted path keeps away from the edge of any precipice and does not involve any real danger.

Start by the electricity generating station at Urdón, on the N621 in the gorge of La Hermida, approximately 10 kilometres south of Panes. There is room for a few cars to park on the side of the road, and also in the track which leads west from the road. It is on the border of Asturias and Cantabria. Park here, and follow the track to the west, away from the road.

Almost immediately take a right fork to go to the right of the hydroelectric works, and then cross a bridge over the river Urdón. Follow the path with the stream to your right. Cross a bridge over a watercourse, then cross another bridge over the river and soon begin to ascend, leaving the stream below on the left. The path zigzags upwards, ascending a gully, and eventually passes to the far side of the gully to reach a broad shoulder above a fall to the stream. This balcony, La Bargona, gives a view of the gorge below. The path goes round the nose of the hill and reaches an open area with a pylon, which supplies power to the village above.

- From here the path gains height in more zigzags. The views down into the gorge below are spectacular. A series of major bends soon follows. You can see them ahead, and they look daunting. But the going is gradual, and it is a steady ascent rather than a major challenge. This area is known as the Balcon de Pilatos (Pilate's Balcony).

- Shortly after the end of the main ascent you will pass a few huts (animal winterings) and a little higher up you will begin to see the village. To reach it you must skirt round the top of a valley, and then pass cabins with a *fuente* (a spring), before ascending again and finally crossing hay meadows to reach the village, where you will find a bar/shop for refreshments before you return by the outward route.

For the return there is little option, unless you left a car at Tresviso to begin with. There is an occasional bus, but the journey from Tresviso to Urdón is long and complex. The footpath is the only normal option.

GPS REFERENCES (UTM)

Start and finish	367549 4791784
Balcon de Pilatos	366182 4790883
Tresviso village	364604 4790740

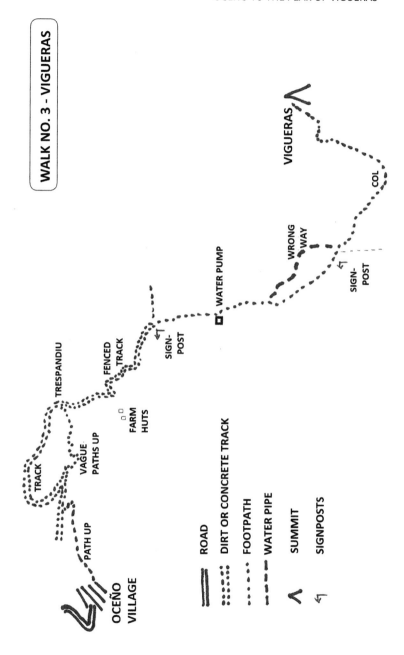

WALK NO. 3 - VIGUERAS

VIGUERAS

COL

WRONG WAY

SIGN-POST

WATER PUMP

TRESPANDIU

FENCED TRACK

SIGN-POST

TRACK

VAGUE PATHS UP

FARM HUTS

PATH UP

OCEÑO VILLAGE

ROAD

DIRT OR CONCRETE TRACK

FOOTPATH

WATER PIPE

SUMMIT

SIGNPOSTS

WALK NO. 3

OCEÑO TO THE PEAK OF VIGUERAS

Vigueras is one of the smaller peaks of the Picos de Europa, but its ascent makes a lovely walk with great views of the central peaks, and Vigueras itself sits above a spectacular precipice.

Distance	15 km round trip
Ascent	1,050 metres
Overall grade	Moderate
Terrain	Good paths and tracks, plus a little scratchy undergrowth.
Exposure	A drop to one side of the summit.
Highest point	1,313 metres

Oceño is a farming hamlet at 500 metres above sea level, and 300 metres above the road from Panes to Arenas de Cabrales. Drive west from Panes on the C6312 and take a left turn at the hamlet of Mildón, which has a signpost to Oceño. After ascending steeply round some sharp bends, park on the right side of the road immediately before the village.

- Walk straight through the village, going just north of east. At the top of the village take a mule track/ footpath, which soon reaches a *fuente* and swings right and then left again. After half a kilometre the path goes through a gate on to a concrete road. Follow the road uphill. It very soon swings right. Some 250 metres after that bend, at a junction of tracks, you have a choice. The easiest route is to go left and to stay on the concrete track until it reaches meadows and a *fuente* at Trespandiu. The alternative is more interesting but harder to find. It is as follows.

- Where the main track swings left, leave it and go downhill slightly on a track to the right. At the next bend take a track going uphill to the left, keeping to the right-hand (southern) side of the main valley.

- Take this track up the right side of the valley. It leads uphill, and passes one or two old farm buildings. There are some minor tracks, so you need to follow your instincts rather than a set route. Keep going on cattle tracks and grassy areas, aiming generally to the east and uphill. You may encounter some prickly stretches, but you should gradually ascend and reach the meadow and the *fuente* on the col of Trespandiu.

- At Trespandiu, turn right. The concrete track from the village continues uphill, going south in zigzags. There are paths that you can use as shortcuts to avoid the bends, including one shortly before some farm buildings. Follow the track, either on the track itself or on the shortcuts, as it continues uphill. Views of the valley of the Rubó open up to your left. The track levels out, with a rustic fence to one side, and when it starts to descend, follow it to the very end, where some signposts indicate the way to San Esteban and Tresviso.

- Go straight on to cross the grassy meadow, following the signpost. At the far end of the meadow ascend a path on a grassy slope to reach a col with a small building, which houses a water pump. Beyond here a good footpath continues, contouring to the south.

- Follow the path, and at a junction take the right fork to reach the top of a delightful ridge with superb views to the central Picos. As the path crosses to the south side of the ridge, follow it to another col (Collada Llamea), where the signposted Tresviso route departs from the San Esteban route. Go left, following the San Esteban sign. Descend slightly, and then some cattle tracks go to the right along the side of the valley, the bottom of which gradually rises to meet you. In case of any navigational difficulty, you can descend to the bottom of the valley and follow it uphill, all the way to the top at the col of Tamandón.

- This col makes a good resting place, with great views. There is a watering hole there, so it is frequented by cattle and horses. From the col, simply ascend to the left (north-east) to reach the peak. There is no footpath as such, but there are cattle tracks. The best route is to keep to the right, near a wire fence. There is a false summit, from which the trig point on the main peak of Vigueras can be seen. The right-hand edge of the summit ridge is a precipice with terrific views down. But those of a nervous disposition can avoid it easily enough, as the other side consists of gentle slopes.

- Return by the outward route.

There is a possible variation, for which you would need to leave a vehicle at the village of San Esteban, near Panes:

To descend to San Esteban, having descended from Vigueras to the Tamandón col, instead of turning right (north-west) to return to the start, turn left into the valley below and follow the valley all the way down to San Esteban. There is a partly overgrown path which keeps to the left, parallel with the stream below.

If returning by the outward route, at GPS 361462 4793394 you will meet a minor path which skirts the right-hand (east) side of the hill. But be warned: this is the route of a water pipe, not a footpath. It involves a narrow stretch with some exposure. Avoid this and stay on the main path.

When you reach the *fuente* at Trespandiu, you can simply walk down the concrete track all the way to the village.

GPS REFERENCES (UTM)

Start and finish	359055 4795314
Track Junction	359889 4795538
Trespandiu	360447 4795555
Water pump	361174 4793821
Collada Llamea	361462 4793394
Summit	362649 4793632

Pool above the Andara refuge – **WALKS 6 & 10**

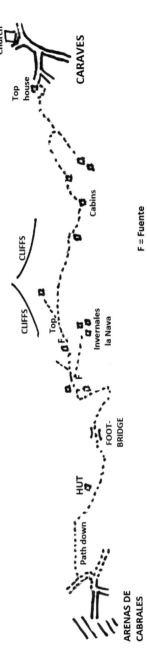

WALK NO. 4 - CÁRAVES TO ARENAS

Church

CARAVES

Top house

Cabins

F = Fuente

CLIFFS

CLIFFS

Top

F

Invernales
la Nava

F

FOOT-
BRIDGE

HUT

Path down

ARENAS DE
CABRALES

WALK NO. 4

CÁRAVES TO ARENAS DE CABRALES

Arenas is a small, lively town at the northern edge of the Picos de Europa, and a gateway into the higher mountains. Here is a very good walk which ends in the town itself: not too difficult, yet giving a flavour of the higher hills. It is a linear walk along the length of the Sierra de Juan Robre, so it needs a car at each end or a taxi ride back to the start.

Distance	10 km linear
Ascent	870 metres
Overall grade	Moderate
Terrain	Good paths and fields
Exposure	Nil
Highest point	825 metres

Start the walk at the village of Cáraves, which is to the north side of the C6312. Turn off the main road west of Trescares, where Cáraves is signposted. Drive up the narrow road to reach the village. At a junction take the right fork and park near the church, where there is room for four or five cars.

- Walk from the church back down the road and take the right fork up to the higher part of the village. Take the next right fork and go to the very highest house. Go to the left-hand side of the house and turn right and then left at the back of the house to take a track that ascends gradually to the west through trees.

- Continue along the path until after ten minutes or so you reach a right turn on to a footpath uphill. (If you miss the turn and reach some ruined cabins you have gone too far.)

35

- Take the right turn and follow the path gradually uphill. If you have difficulty following the path, traverse the fields and woods going south of west and staying well below the cliffs that are above on your right. The path continues in gradual ascent, crossing fields and passing through patches of woods to reach a col with a cabin. Continue above the cabin and keep ascending to another col with another cabin.

- From the cabin ascend to the right and then go left and gradually up, and traverse above a big, broad gully. The path goes just below the rock wall that stands above the top of the gully. You will reach a *majada* (a meadow, with two cabins), and further on another, broader gully. Cross the gully high up, getting closer to the escarpment above, and follow the path that goes towards the Collado de las Arnias, which you can see higher up again. Keep well to the left of a cabin at this high col, which is the highest point of the walk.

- Below and ahead there is another *majada*, with several cabins. These are the Invernales de la Nava (animal wintering). The path does not descend to la Nava, but continues at a higher level on the right, passing an old *fuente* and another cabin. After crossing more meadows you will encounter a route coming in from the right, marked with red paint. Go straight on, past another *fuente*, and continue past another cabin. After crossing a small rocky area, the path swings left and starts to zigzag down the western slopes of the sierra towards Arenas. After the zigzags, cross a small bridge, pass a *fuente* and a hut, and you will soon enter holm oak woods by a fence with a makeshift gate. At a junction of paths by the gate, take the left fork. Descend and then turn left on a broad track, which leads you past a cheese factory into the town of Arenas de Cabrales.

GPS REFERENCES (UTM)

Start	359960 4797382
Collado las Arnias	356300 4796893
Top of zigzags	355770 4796065
Arenas	352811 4796004

A brave "Rebeco" deer – **WALK 6**

WALK NO. 5 - PICA FUENTE SOLES

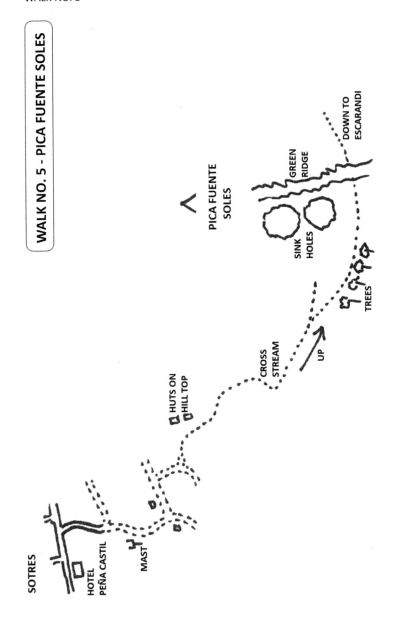

WALK NO. 5

SOTRES TO PICA FUENTE SOLES
(1,564 metres altitude)

A minor but splendid peak, overlooking the village of Sotres. A short walk with some steep ground.

Distance	6 km round trip
Ascent	560 metres
Overall grade	Easy
Terrain	Tracks and paths plus some muddy and scratchy sections.
Exposure	Nil
Highest point	1,564 metres

I grade this walk as easy due to its short distance. Otherwise it involves everything that you would expect from a mountain walk. It is a good ascent to a lovely peak overlooking the village.

- In Sotres, from Hotel Peña Castil, walk up the street. Turn right just before Casa Cipriano. Follow this road uphill. Go past a radio/telephone mast on the right. Fork right at a junction of tracks. You will find a bench with a brilliant view over the Duje valley. Keep going on the track. Pass a cabin on the right. Ignore a turn to the right, and follow the track to the left. Pass another cabin on the left as you cross a meadow. About 200 metres past this cabin take a track uphill to your right.

- The track soon becomes grassy. When it takes a sharp turn to the right, turn left on a bit of concrete track. It swings to the right again, passing below a cabin on top of a rocky hillside to your left. While crossing a grassy area, a vague path takes you uphill towards beech woods, keeping to the right side of a hill. The path soon swings right, crossing a small, muddy stream. At some times of year the mud here can be very clingy. It then continues uphill and follows the right-hand side of a valley through trees, to reach an open area before more trees in a valley beyond.

- It is easy to go astray here. There is a path ahead, but the correct path is slightly to the right-hand side of the open area, marked by a small cairn. It is a narrow path, and takes you uphill slightly to the right, skirting the woods on the side of the hill. Follow this path all the way uphill to reach the top of a rise with an open grassy area, and a green valley in front and to your left. This is the Hoyo (Hole) de Fuente Soles. The peak is on the other side of the hole. All you need to do is skirt round the hole on rough ground, and make your way to the top as best you can. There are two peaks. The highest point is the western one.

- Return to Sotres by the way you came.

GPS REFERENCES (UTM)

Start	358024 4788129
Start of stream valley	358565 4787568
Col above the Hoyo	359721 4787342
Summit	359722 4787728

WALK NO. 6 - CUETU TEJAU

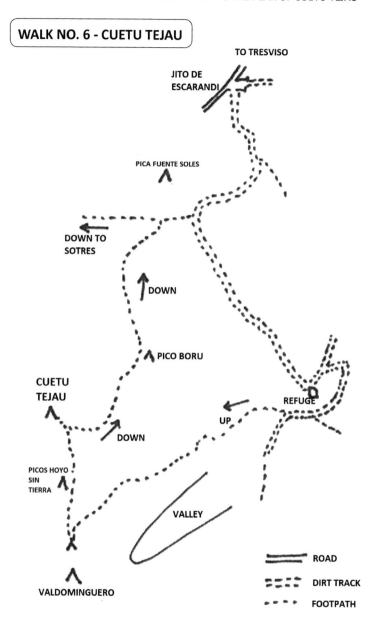

TO TRESVISO

JITO DE ESCARANDI

PICA FUENTE SOLES

DOWN TO SOTRES

DOWN

PICO BORU

CUETU TEJAU

DOWN

REFUGE

UP

PICOS HOYO SIN TIERRA

VALLEY

VALDOMINGUERO

ROAD

DIRT TRACK

FOOTPATH

WALK NO. 6

ESCARANDI TO THE PEAK OF CUETU TEJAU
(2,129 metres altitude)

A circuit of high peaks.

Distance	14 km
Ascent	1,100 metres
Overall grade	Strenuous
Terrain	Footpaths and some boulders.
Exposure	Only at the very summit.
Highest point	2,207 metres

Cuetu Tejau is the dominant peak south-east of Sotres, a village at 1,045 metres altitude. The ascent from Sotres is 1,084 metres in a distance of only 5 kilometres. Despite the formidable appearance of the north-west face, there is no technical difficulty. The final ascent to the peak involves some easy boulder scrambling. The peak has a view straight back down to Sotres. This circular route also visits neighbouring peaks. Starting at the car park at Jito de Escarandi, 3 km from Sotres, saves 250 metres of ascent.

- From the car park, take the right-hand track of two major dirt tracks, signposted to the Casetón de Andara (a mountain refuge). Ignore a turn down to the right. After ten minutes, pass a footpath going downhill to the left, and stay on the main track. (I use that path in another of these walks.) The track ascends gradually to reach the Andara refuge after about an hour's easy walking.

- From the refuge, ascend the scree-covered hillside to the south. There are several very loose paths. The easiest route is to turn left at the front door of the refuge. Go along a level track and take the first stony track up to the right. It will lead you to a level area, where you are looking down to the right on to the refuge. Continue to reach a pond with red rocks. From here paths go in all directions. Take a path to the west to enter a valley.

- After just a few metres there is a junction. One track goes off to the left. Another goes ahead into the valley. Ignore these and take a footpath to the right that ascends towards the northern ridge. Follow the ridge on cattle tracks or over grass, and you will gradually ascend above the valley, which should be below to your left. (*The valley is the Pozo de Andara, which was a lake until emptied by mining 100 years ago. It is planned to restore it for its 2018 centenary.*) Following the top of the ridge will lead you in a generally south-westerly direction. You will need to navigate your way along as best you can, as there is no clear path. Ascend and descend several times. The objective is to stay as close as you safely can to the edge of the ridgeline, but you will need to leave it at times. Look for the safest route while staying parallel with the ridge.

- Continue ascending to reach the peaks of Campos de los Senderos at 2,161 metres and 2,179 metres, and keep going south-west towards the highest peak in this section, Valdominguero. Before reaching the main peak of Valdominguero, you will reach a subsidiary top at 2,207 metres, from where it is difficult to see your way to the main summit. So forget it. (Walk 16 of this collection goes there, but this walk goes in the opposite direction.) Turn right (north) and follow the new ridgeline, with views down into the Duje valley on your left.

- Again, there is danger to the left but none to the right, where the slopes are gentler. Simply follow the ridgeline, which will lead you to the next top at Picas de Jou sin Tierre (the Peaks of the Bottomless Hole), the said hole being down below to your right. This peak is marked with a cairn, and from there follow the ridge again to reach the final cairn at the summit of Cuetu Tejau (2,129 metres). The views are brilliant in all directions. The ground is bare rock, slabs and boulders.

- From the summit, descend over boulders going to the east and heading for a valley. Once in the centre of the valley you will find a footpath that has come down from the Bottomless Hole. Follow the path downhill to the north. It will lead you to a minor hilltop at Pico Boru – but keep left, below the hilltop. The path splits at times. You may find a memorial to victims of an air crash (the wreckage was still lying around until 2014), but if you miss it don't worry. Keep to the path marked by cairns. Don't be in a hurry to go downhill to the left, but look for two hills ahead and follow the path between them, from where it will lead you down more steeply in zigzags to reach a green col ahead of the Pica de Fuente Soles.

- Turning left here would lead you back down to Sotres, but taking a path down to the right leads you through cattle pastures to reach the dirt track you ascended early in the walk. Turn left along the track to return to Escarandi.

GPS REFERENCES (UTM)

Start	360439 4788579
Andara refuge	360904 4786019
Path up	360714 4785852
Campos de los Senderos	359086 4784993
Picas del Jou sin Tierre	358914 4785199
Cuetu Tejau	358919 4785832
Col (turn right)	359721 4787342

WALK NO. 7 - SOTRES/TIELVE CIRCUIT

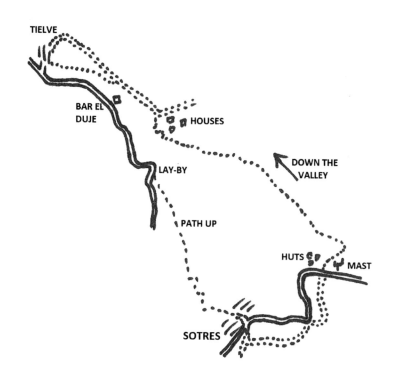

TIELVE

BAR EL
DUJE

HOUSES

LAY-BY

DOWN THE
VALLEY

PATH UP

HUTS

MAST

SOTRES

WALK NO. 7

CIRCUIT FROM SOTRES VIA TIELVE

A delightful walk between two villages that descends a green valley with good views, and returns by an ancient mule track.

Distance	13 km
Ascent	900 metres
Overall grade	Moderate
Terrain	Good footpaths and a little road walking.
Exposure	Nil
Highest point	1,237 metres

(As a one-way walk, with transport back from Tielve, it is easy, with an ascent of only 200 metres.)

- In Sotres, walk up the street from Hotel Peña Castil and turn right on the street before Casa Cipriano. At the first junction of tracks turn left. Continue to another junction close to a road, and take the right fork on a track uphill. Continue up here until you reach the road once more at the *majada* (huts) of La Caballar. Cross the road and make for a radio antenna on the far side. A path begins here, going firstly to the north, down into a valley, and reaches a *fuente* (a water tap and an animal trough), where the route turns left and proceeds down the valley bottom. There are animal tracks here, so the main path may not be obvious, but keep going and the path (marked with yellow and white paint) should become clear.

- Stay in the valley as it narrows, and until it emerges into the open, with views opening up to the left towards the Central massif of the Picos. (Eventually, in clear weather, you should have a good view of Picu Urriellu, the most emblematic of the Picos.) Keep going until you join a broader track, which will bring you to some farmhouses at Majada Tobao. Beyond the houses take the track to the left. It will take you all the way to Tielve, but after about 0.75 km look for a footpath on the left that descends more steeply and is more interesting.

- Go down to pass through the small village. There is a bar, but opening times are spasmodic. Continue down to the main road, and turn left up the road towards Sotres. You will soon reach the Bar Duje, which is normally open and makes a good place for refreshments.

If you want an easy day you can take a taxi back to Sotres for just a few euros, or if you have two vehicles, leave one at each end. (*If in difficulty ask the owners at El Duje.*)

On leaving the bar, walk up the road back towards Sotres for 1.5 kilometres. Pass a parking area on the right, and you will see that soon the old road makes a loop to the left. It is now a lay-by. Just on the far (south-eastern) side of this loop is the start of a path, signposted to Sotres. It is the old mule trail between the two villages, dating from before the present road. The path climbs above the road, and leads you directly back to Sotres, with increasingly good views of Peña Main and the Duje valley as you ascend.

GPS REFERENCES (UTM)

Start and finish	358024 4788129
La Caballar	358993 4788647
Fuente	359274 4788755
Tielve	355856 4791530
Start of path up	357016 4790240

WALK NO. 8 - SOTRES - PEÑA MAIN - TIELVE

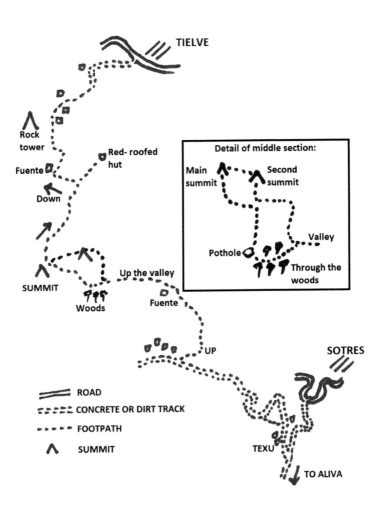

TIELVE

Rock tower

Red-roofed hut

Fuente

Down

Detail of middle section:

Main summit

Second summit

Valley

Pothole

Through the woods

Up the valley

SUMMIT

Woods

Fuente

UP

SOTRES

TEXU

TO ALIVA

═══ ROAD

▪▪▪▪▪ CONCRETE OR DIRT TRACK

••••• FOOTPATH

∧ SUMMIT

WALK NO. 8

SOTRES TO PEÑA MAIN AND TIELVE

A linear walk to a peak outside the Central massif, with terrific views into the Central massif itself.

Distance	11 km
Ascent	800 metres
Overall grade	Moderate
Terrain	Footpaths, woods, limestone boulders and a just a little road walking.
Exposure	Virtually nil
Highest point	1,605 metres

The principal walk is one-way. The return from Tielve to Sotres can be made by taxi, or by walking the second part of Walk 7, a distance of about 6 km. A second option, which is to complete a circuit and return to the start, follows below.

- From Sotres, leave the village by walking down the main road and round some bends. Where the road swings sharply to the right, go straight ahead on a dirt road, which is signposted to Aliva. It descends and then swings to the right. It then swings back to the left. Look for a footpath here that goes down to reach the red roofs of the Invernales del Texu (winter sheds). If you miss the path just continue on the track and take the first right turn.

- The concrete track at the bottom of the valley goes uphill in zigzags. You can follow the track or, alternatively, take a much steeper shortcut up a footpath that starts right at the bottom and cuts out most of the bends. Where the footpath rejoins the track, continue on the track going generally west.

- After levelling out, and becoming a dirt track, the road swings right at a junction. Then it swings left to reach a *majada* (a group of houses and cabins). When you reach the very first of these buildings, turn right up to the cabin, go through a makeshift gate, and look for a footpath going uphill to the right behind the hut. After some zigzags this will lead you round the eastern side of the cliffs above, and then in a generally north-westerly direction uphill. The path levels and then descends towards a valley with cabins.

- The path leads across towards a rocky area above and to the right of the valley bottom, and then starts to ascend again, going steadily uphill. After the first ascent you will continue with woods on your left. The path is marked with cairns and red paint. Towards the top end of the woods you will pass a solitary tree standing out from the rest. A few metres beyond it there is a large cairn, beyond which the main path swings to the right. But prepare to leave the main path here. Just past the cairn take a vague path to the left, which ascends through the trees.

- Just before the top of the woods there is a small gully with a cave to the right, which is used for curing cheeses. But it is well hidden and you may miss it. The next landmark, as you emerge from the woods, is a deep pothole shaft going vertically down. (The GPS reference is approximately 355610 4789084.) Take care. It is dangerous. Here you should turn right to follow cairns up the hill. There is a path at times, but it is not easy to follow. However, your target is the very top of the hill, so if you lose the path, just keep going up, taking care to avoid stumbling over the limestone rocks and the heather. There are two summits. The higher one, Cabeza de la Mesa, is the left (western) peak. As it comes into view, keep left, cross to the left side of a depression between the two tops and take a footpath marked with cairns to the summit. There is a trig point, and a fabulous view of the Naranjo de Bulnes mountain. You may be able to see the Urriellu refuge at its base.

DESCENT OPTION ONE – TO TIELVE:

- From the summit, face north and look for a red-roofed cabin in the distance. That is your next target. While skirting to the north side of the lower peak, find a path on the right-hand side of a depression. It leads you gradually down into the valley, towards woods. Then it takes you through the woods and through a hollow to a point shortly before the red-roofed cabin, when the path swings downhill to the left. (If you reach the cabin, go back for a couple of hundred metres and you should find it.) The path now leads gradually downhill to the west, mainly through woodland, but sometimes in the open. It crosses watercourses and can be muddy and slippery in some places. At the time of writing (2016) the path, although marked with cairns and red paint, is becoming somewhat overgrown, so you may have to push through or avoid small beech saplings.

- The path will lead you to a *fuente* (a spring and a tank), which is a good place for a rest. The path goes to the right here, and continues to reach a point above a meadow with a wonderful limestone pinnacle on the left beyond it. Follow this meadow downhill, keeping well to the right of the pinnacle. Make your way across diagonally to the right and look for some cabins below the trees. From there a track commences, which will lead you down to a bridge over the Duje river and the road. At a junction of tracks, keep right. Then turn right on the road and within five minutes or so you will arrive the Bar Duje, the end of this walk. If you wish to walk back to Sotres, follow the route described in the Walk 7, the Sotres to Tielve circuit.

DESCENT OPTION TWO – CIRCUIT BACK TO THE START:

- From the trig point at the summit, descend to cross a broad ridge heading directly to the lower summit (Cabeza Quemado), marked with a large cairn.

- Keep going straight on, following the cairns, which will lead you to a point you had already visited on the ascent. Go to the left here to follow more cairns downhill. Unless you find a different route from mine you will soon have to make a slightly difficult scramble down sharp limestone.

- Below the limestone crags, follow the cairns again as they swing downhill to the right. There is a good path here, and after crossing a small ridge it will lead you down directly to the lone tree where you turned into the woods earlier in the walk.

- Descend the valley on the path with the cairns until you reach the rocks above the meadow with huts. Stay high and cross above the meadow, but do not continue straight ahead. Keep over to the right of the next hilltop, and cross a small col to descend the path you ascended earlier, and go down to the hut with a gate. Return to Sotres along the dirt road to the left.

GPS REFERENCES (UTM)

Start	358024 4788129
Path up to the right	356161 4788271
Majada	355980 4788619
Pothole	355610 4789084
Summit	354677 4789349
Go left	355060 4789945
Keep right of limestone peak	354831 4790766
Tielve (Bar El Duje)	356404 4791290

WALK NO. 9 - LA JUNCIANA, SAGRADO CORAZÓN AND SAMELAR

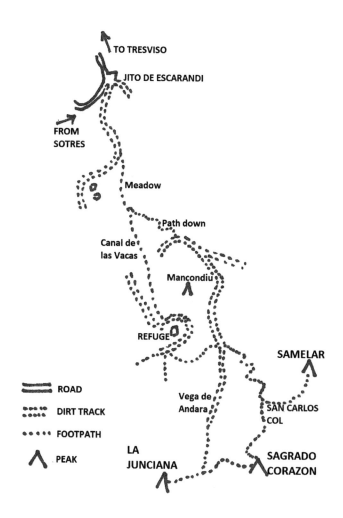

TO TRESVISO

JITO DE ESCARANDI

FROM SOTRES

Meadow

Path down

Canal de las Vacas

Mancondiu

REFUGE

SAMELAR

ROAD

DIRT TRACK

FOOTPATH

PEAK

Vega de Andara

SAN CARLOS COL

LA JUNCIANA

SAGRADO CORAZON

WALK NO. 9

THREE PEAKS OF LA JUNCIANA, SAGRADO CORAZÓN AND SAMELAR

A choice of one, two or three peaks in the Eastern massif, with great views of the massif and of the Liébana valley below.

Distance	17 km
Ascent	1,350 metres
Overall grade	Strenuous, with moderate options
Terrain	Footpaths and limestone slabs
Exposure	Virtually nil
Highest point	2,227 metres

La Junciana (2,202 metres), Sagrado Corazón (2,214 metres) and Samelar (2,227 metres) are neighbouring peaks, on either side of the San Carlos col, towards the north-eastern end of the Andara (Eastern) massif. The three tops can be done in a single, strenuous excursion. The focal point for all three mountains is the Vega de Andara, from where any of them can be accessed if you choose not to do all three. The above statistics relate to the complete circuit.

This walk begins and ends at el Jito de Escarandi, 3 km from Sotres towards Tresviso.

- From the car park at Escarandi (1,291 metres) take the dirt track south, uphill and signposted for the Refugio de Andara, which is our first target. The conventional route is along the track, but this route is more interesting. Take the track at first, but after ten minutes, when the track veers to the left and then to the right, take a footpath going downhill to your left. You will descend to a lovely meadow.

- Go straight along the meadow, and after about 100 metres, you will see some cabins over towards the right. Do not go to the cabins, but go straight on and take a path uphill keeping just to the left of a valley bottom (the Canal de las Vacas). It as an old mule trail, as you can see by the rocks that mark the side of the trail. The path divides at times, but the object is to gradually ascend alongside or in the valley. It is difficult to describe the exact route, but not so difficult to follow the path. If you lose it don't worry, because the refuge is at the very top of the main valley.

- During this ascent the huge limestone wall of Mancondiu is to your left. You will reach a boulder field. The path zigzags to get past the boulders. The path now swings all over the place, but you can take a shortcut and go straight up the valley. You will soon see ahead of you a spoil heap from old mines, and on arriving there you will see the refuge itself at the top of a steep shale slope. The refuge (smartly repainted in 2017) is manned in the summer, but sometimes there is nobody there, so you may or may not get a coffee.

- Facing the refuge door, turn left along a level track, and then go up to the right at the first opportunity. There are stony paths going up in zigzags. Take any of them, but keep going uphill and to the right to reach a point where you can see the refuge below to your right. Five minutes after leaving the refuge you will find a level area with, at the far end, a small pond at the beginning of a valley leading to the west. (The pond may be dry.) Do not go into the valley to the west, and do not go uphill towards a green fence. Instead take a path to the east, and ascend to reach a col at the southern base of Mancondiu. After crossing the col, follow the path along the hillside and then down to reach a broad track with the Vega de Andara to your right.

- Turn right on the track towards the vega.

- For La Junciana and the complete circuit, continue straight ahead on the track with the vega to your right and ancient lead mine ruins all around.

If you want to avoid La Junciana, take a track which goes uphill to your left. The track soon narrows to a footpath and ascends in zigzags, steadily climbing all the way to the col of San Carlos (2,052 metres). From there a path leads across the top of a huge gully and up the far side to the summit of Sagrado Corazón.

- La Junciana is the peak above the valley to the south-west. There is no clear path. To ascend the peak, follow the mine tracks to the south of the vega and then leave the tracks and ascend over limestone rocks to reach the ridge ahead, from where a cairned route to the right leads you easily enough to the summit. There are red rocks here, which I imagine contain iron, but I am not an expert. From the summit, retrace your steps to the east and back to the broad ridge, but instead of descending to the north, stay on the ridge and walk up to the second summit, Sagrado Corazón.

- *The name Sagrado Corazón means 'Sacred Heart'. There is a statue of Jesus on the summit, and an annual pilgrimage. The traditional name of the mountain is in fact Pico San Carlos. Many mountains here have two or even three names.*

- From the top of Sagrado Corazón go north, below a col that separates the summit from a secondary top. Then follow a path downhill to the top of the huge San Carlos gully. To ascend Samelar, simply follow the rise from the col, keeping the San Carlos gully to your right for half a kilometre. From the summit you have good views to the eastern end of the national park and of the coastline to the north-east.

- Return to the San Carlos col, and turn right downhill. The path zigzags, but there are options to take shortcuts on open ground. Follow the path back to the track on the edge of the Vega de Andara and turn right along the track. Do not turn left on the footpath back to the refuge. Instead, stay on the track to skirt round the east and then the north side of Mancondiu. The track makes some twists and turns and is eventually joined by another track coming up from the right side, with a semicircular wall at the junction. Keep straight ahead at the junction, hugging close to the mountainside. Almost immediately after the junction of tracks, a footpath goes downhill to the right. Follow this path. Very shortly, at a junction where a path goes to the right, go straight on.

• Once on the path, while looking straight ahead you can see in the distance the main track from the refuge back to Escarandi, and a red-roofed cabin below it. That is your next target. The path is intermittent, but you should be able to follow it. If in doubt, don't lose height down to the right too quickly and keep aiming for the red-roofed cabin. You will soon the reach the meadow below the cabin, which you will recognise from having been there earlier in the day. Walk across the length of the meadow, and take the footpath going uphill to the left, which takes you to the main track, which you should follow to the right to get back in a few minutes more to Escarandi.

GPS REFERENCES (UTM)

Start	360442 4788588
Andara refuge	360912 4786019
Mancondiu col	361275 4785760
San Carlos col	361941 4784898
Sagrado Corazón	361861 4784282

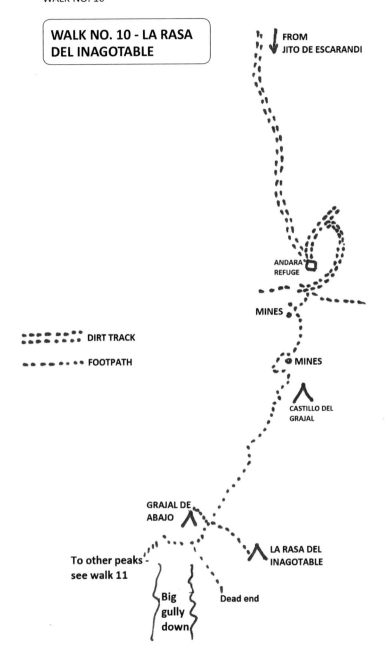

WALK NO. 10 - LA RASA DEL INAGOTABLE

FROM JITO DE ESCARANDI

ANDARA REFUGE

MINES

DIRT TRACK

FOOTPATH

MINES

CASTILLO DEL GRAJAL

GRAJAL DE ABAJO

LA RASA DEL INAGOTABLE

To other peaks - see walk 11

Big gully down

Dead end

WALK NO. 10

ESCARANDI TO LA RASA DEL INAGOTABLE (2,282 metres) AND GRAJAL DE ABAJO (2,246 metres)

An ascent to two peaks of the Eastern massif.

Distance	15 km
Ascent	1,150 metres
Overall grade	Moderate, plus options
Terrain	Footpaths and shale
Exposure	Take care on La Rasa del Inagotable summit. Otherwise there is no problem.
Highest point	2,282 metres

• Start at the car park at el Jito de Escarandi, 3 km from Sotres. Take the uphill dirt track, signposted to the Refugio de Andara, and follow it for an hour to reach the refuge. If it is manned you may get a coffee. Facing the refuge door, take a track to the left, but turn right uphill as soon as you can, and zigzag upwards until you see the refuge below. Continue upwards to reach a level area with a pond (often dry in summer and autumn) where a number of paths head off in different directions. Turn left and then turn right again almost immediately (south and uphill) to pass some old mineshafts protected by green fencing.

• Follow the path beyond the mineshafts, and then swing sharply right, passing an open mineshaft on the left. The track leads you up and to the right-hand (western) side of the peak of El Castillo del Grajal, which from below vaguely resembles a fortification. Beyond there the track continues in zigzags. Avoid any turn-offs to the right that might lead you to the valley below. Continue ascending to reach a col (the Collado del Mojón) at 2,200 metres altitude.

- From here, go to the left for a steady but non-technical walk up a stony slope to reach the summit of La Rasa del Inagotable. Take care at the summit, as there is a vertical drop of some 200 metres at the other side. Return to Collado del Mojón and then go west, and in only 200 metres of distance and 50 metres of ascent you will reach the attractive and easy peak of Grajal de Abajo (2,248 metres).

- You can then return to Escarandi by the way you came. But you also have the strenuous option to ascend one or more of Picu Jierru, Picas del Jierru, La Morra de Lechugales or Silla del Caballo Cimero. See Walk 11 for more details.

- Whichever of these options you choose, you will need to retrace your steps to the Collado del Mojón, the Andara refuge and thence to Escarandi.

GPS REFERENCES (UTM)

Start	360442 4788588
Andara refuge	360912 4786019
Collado del Mojón	360358 4784475
La Rasa del Inagotable summit	360662 4784270

WALK NO. 11 - SILLA DEL CABALLO CIMERO

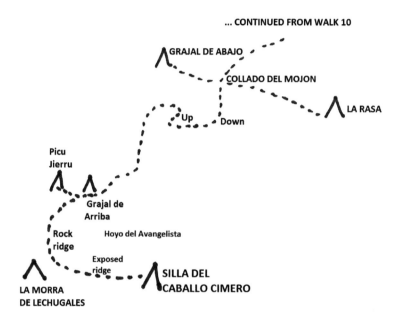

WALK NO. 11

JITO DE ESCARANDI TO SILLA DEL CABALLO CIMERO (2,436 metres)

An ascent to one of the highest peaks in the Eastern massif.

Distance	18 km
Ascent	1,350 metres
Overall grade	Strenuous
Terrain	Footpaths and a narrow ridge
Exposure	The final approach is very exposed.
Highest point	2,436 metres

The final section is along a narrow, rocky ridge, and is suitable for experienced hill walkers only.

The walk is an extended version of Walk 10, leading to the highest section of the Andara (Eastern) massif.

Begin at Jito de Escarandi, walk up to the Andara refuge and continue to the Collado del Mojón, as described in Walk 10, and then do as follows:

- On reaching Collado del Mojón, keep straight on, going south and slightly downhill. Take a path to the right, which skirts around the southern flanks of the peak of Grajal de Abajo. The path soon ascends steeply and crosses to the far side of a short ridge. Follow the path along that ridge until a turn to the left and a short ascent bring you back to the south side of the broad ridgetop.

- The path now becomes easy, taking an almost level route until a point where it swings sharp left. Do not follow the track to the left. Instead go straight ahead into a green valley and then go straight up the valley, keeping the top of the ridge over to your right.

- As the ground rises and becomes rocky, cairns will lead you over the peak of Grajal de Arriba, where you have great views of most of the Picos, and of the Pozo de Valdominguero below to the right. Keep straight ahead now, on a narrow ridge. It looks precipitous, but cairns and paint marks will keep you away from danger on this section.

- Ahead of you and somewhat to the right, the next peak is Picu Jierru. If you wish, you can make this your destination and return to the start. It will have been a great day out. But there are higher peaks ahead and to the left. To do them, do not ascend to Picu Jierru. Instead, stay on a path below and to the left of this summit. It is a vague 'trod' in places and may be hard to follow. But keep going gradually upwards to reach the top of the ridge which connects Picu Jierru to the next peak, which is (confusingly) called Picas de Jierru.

- Walk along the crest of this short ridge, which is broad and presents no problems. At the far end of the ridge, ignore another path going up to the right and follow the lower path to the left, as it circuits round the top of the massive depression of the Hoyo del Evangelista.

- Now the narrow ridge commences. It is a scramble on generally good rock, ascending and descending at times. You may need to use hands, feet and bottoms. It is not the most difficult of scrambles, technically, but it is exposed on both sides. Take care.

- As you leave the ridge at the far end, all that remains is to walk up the last few metres to the summit.

At the summit, the peaks you can see include:

In the Eastern massif, from the left looking east: Picos de Cámara; Prao Cortes; Cortes; La Morra de Lechugales (the highest); Picas del Jierru; Pico Jierru; Grajal de Arriba; La Rasa del Inagotable; La Junciana; Sagrado Corazón, and others.

In the Central massif:
Peña Vieja; Picos de Santa Ana; Marta Navarra; El Escamellau; Picu Urriellu; Peña Castil, and others.

- Return to Jito de Escarandi by the outward route.

GPS REFERENCES (UTM)

Collado del Mojón	360358 4784475
Grajal de Arriba	359535 4783925
Picu Jierru	359150 4783844
First ridge	359150 4783844
Silla del Caballo Cimero	359467 4783451

Caballo Cimero – **WALK 11**

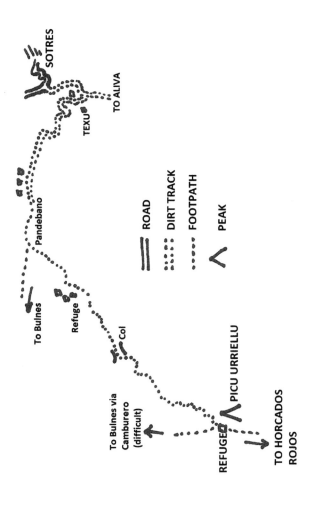

WALK NO. 12 - FIRST PART TO URRIELLU

SOTRES

TO ALIVA

TEXU

Pandebano

ROAD

DIRT TRACK

FOOTPATH

PEAK

To Bulnes

Refuge

Col

To Bulnes via
Camburero
(difficult)

PICU URRIELLU

REFUGE

TO HORCADOS
ROJOS

WALK NO. 12 - PART 2 - URRIELLU TO ALIVA

WALK NO. 12

VEGA DE URRIELLO, HORCADOS ROJOS AND ALIVA

The classic traverse of the Central massif.

Distance	22 km
Ascent	1,900 metres
Overall grade	Very strenuous
Terrain	Footpaths, boulders and shale
Exposure	Head for heights needed on the second part. The route ascends via a chain.
Highest point	2,370 metres

This traverse begins in Sotres. It is intended to get you the Urriello refuge for lunch, and to the Aliva hotel/refuge for an overnight stay. It is a big day, but you can stay overnight at Urriellu to break the walk into two sections, which would leave time to explore that area. Or stay at the refuge for two nights and conquer one of the nearby peaks.

THE SECOND PART OF THIS TRAVERSE IS FOR EXPERIENCED HILL WALKERS ONLY.

- From Sotres walk down the main road, and where it swings sharp right go straight ahead on a dirt track. Follow it downhill and turn right to go down to the Invernales del Texu (cattle winterings). Beyond the cabins, a concrete road ascends in zigzags towards the Pandebano pass. At the valley bottom there is a steep footpath on the left that cuts out some bends in the road. As the road levels out it becomes a dirt track. Continue on it, going north-west. Ignore a turning to the left. Pass a group of cabins and houses on the right. You will reach an open area, which is used as a car park.

- The top of the rise ahead is Pandebano. Ascend to the left (south) side of the col. A path then leads to the left towards some houses at 1,315 metres. Pass by them in a south-westerly direction. These houses are in fact the low-level refuge of La Terenosa. Continue on the well-defined path.

- After a further 2 km, you will go left at a narrow col (Collado Vallejo, 1,540 metres) where the landscape changes dramatically from green meadow to rocky mountain. The path undulates, then makes its way uphill, steeply at times, across stony and barren ground, as it goes in zigzags to the base of the Naranjo de Bulnes, the most famous and spectacular peak in the Picos. You will find the Urriello refuge at the base of the mountain, at 1,903 metres above sea level. From mid March onwards the refuge is normally manned, and you can buy lunch and a coffee, a beer or a glass of wine.

- If you have a problem with heights, return the way you came. Otherwise, after leaving the refuge, continue on a good path to the south. It leads you across increasingly barren and remote ground. Keep over to the right to take a zigzag path descending to the Jou sin Tierre (Bottomless Hole). An incline on the left then leads you up and over to the next big hole in the ground, the Jou de los Boches.

- Cross a lunar-like landscape to reach the foot of a cliff at Horcados Rojos. An ascent of the cliff looks impossible, but there is a route, and one route only. It follows a chain, ascending steep and loose ground to reach the top of the precipice. It should be taken with care. It is not technically difficult, but it can be slippery underfoot. It is essential to follow the marked route. Anything else is dangerous. There are gaps in the chain on the less steep sections. Look out for cairns and/or yellow paint at all times. (*In 2017 the chain has become loose in two places. It is still achievable, but more care is needed. I imagine this will soon be repaired.*)

- At the top of the cliff, the chain traverses to the right to reach a broad col, where you turn left downhill and over rocky ground going towards the Verónica refuge which is on a hill ahead. If you have time you can ascend to the refuge for a beer or a coffee. It is not an overnight option. (It is the tiny gun turret of an aircraft carrier. It was deposited up here years ago and has very limited sleeping accommodation. A fantastic place.)

- When coming from Horcados Rojos, turn left at a junction of paths shortly before reaching the Verónica refuge and follow a good path downhill below various peaks. Ignore a path ascending to the left, and continue downhill to reach a junction of tracks at La Vueltona.

- Follow a broad track straight ahead. At the next junction, the right turn leads to the top of the Fuente Dé cable car. But for the Aliva refuge turn left and follow the track down, passing the red-roofed Chalet Real on the left before you get there. There are bends in the track, and a path to the right (at Collado de Juan Toribio) cuts off a lot of the bends and saves distance. The path begins below a sharp, rocky ridge above to your right. Either the path or the track will lead you to the door of the refuge.

The Aliva refuge is in fact a hotel, bar and restaurant, and you can sleep in a single room if you wish – unlike most of the high mountain refuges, which have dormitories. It is an easy walk back to Sotres next day.

From Sotres to Urriellu: 11 km and 1,150 metres ascent.

From Urriellu to Aliva: 11 km and 750 metres ascent.

GPS REFERENCES (UTM)

Start	357963 4788082
Pandebano	354972 4787993
Collado Vallejo	353210 4786710
Urriellu refuge	352027 4784944
Horcados Rojos	351072 4782498
Path junction	350994 4782213
Verónica refuge	350811 4782038
Aliva hotel/refuge	354713 4781006

Vega de Urriellu and the refuge – **WALK 12**

WALK NO. 13 - PEÑA CASTIL

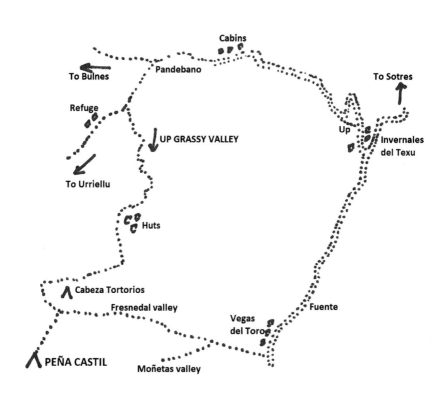

WALK NO. 13

INVERNALES DEL TEXU TO THE PEAK OF PEÑA CASTIL (2,444 metres)

An arduous but rewarding walk to one of the main peaks of the Central massif, with great views to the immediately neighbouring peaks, including the famous Naranjo de Bulnes.

Distance	16 km
Ascent	1,650 metres
Overall grade	Strenuous
Terrain	Footpaths and grassy slopes
Exposure	None
Highest point	2,444 metres

The walk starts and ends at Invernales del Texu, half a kilometre down a dirt road from Sotres. You can park a car there if you drive carefully.

- From the red-roofed cabins start to walk up the concrete road away from Sotres, but look first of all for a path which goes steeply uphill cutting out some of the bends in the road. Continue up the road, and you will see that it soon begins to level out. Ignore a turn to the left and stay on the main track, which swings right and then left again, passing by a group of houses and cabins on the right. You will reach an open area (Pandebano) used commonly as a car park. Keep over to the left and ascend the hill.

- A well-walked path (the route to the Urriellu refuge) goes south-west, towards some houses at the Terenosa refuge. Follow this path a short distance, but before reaching the houses/refuge, turn left off the path and commence a long and strenuous ascent up the Canal de Las Monas, a wide green gully. At the lower end of the "canal" there is no definitive path, but as you ascend a clear path develops. To find it look for two distinct lines of boulders on the hillside above and head for the right hand one of these. You should find a large cairn. A footpath begins there. If you do not immediately find it, walk up the broad gully and you will soon encounter the zigzag path. (The only way I can describe the 'canal' is to say that it is a broad, green valley or gully, and it is the first one to the left of the Urriellu path.)

- Ascend the Canal de Las Monas. On reaching a rocky area keep to the left and enter the narrower gully, which leads you to a group of cabins (the Majada Las Monas) at the top. From here continue on a good footpath towards the west. After passing a small col you should traverse across the northern slopes of a hill (the Cabeza de los Tortorios) until you reach a rocky area at the end of the path, with a drop ahead into a gully. To the left there is a breach in the rocks which allows you to gain access to the Horcada Camburero, a broad col at the base of the Peña Castil peak.

- From here, simply walk up the slope to the southwest to reach the summit. It is no more than a walk all the way, but the views from the top are stunning. The mountain is one of a chain of peaks in a horseshoe, with the Naranjo de Bulnes close by to the west.

- From the summit, return to the Horcada Camburero and turn right, to follow a good path down the Fresnedal gully. This is a long descent, for which few instructions are needed. Simply follow the path all the way down the bottom of the Fresnedal valley, to where it meets a junction with the Monetas valley coming down from the right. Continue downhill to a dirt road at a group of cabins at Vegas del Toro. Turn left on a track to pass the cabins, beyond which there is a *fuente* for nice cool water, and you will soon reach the starting point of the walk at Invernales del Texu, below Sotres.

As you ascend from the Horcada Camburero towards the peak, you may see a series of cairns leading away to the left. For a short diversion, these will lead you to the Cueva del Hielo (the Ice Cave) which is a natural cavern permanently full of snow and ice. Signposts in Spanish warn you that it is dangerous to enter due to the possibility of crevasses. Go to take a look by all means but do not enter.

GPS REFERENCES (UTM)

Invernales del Texu	357376 4787295
Pandebano	354972 4787993
Canal de Las Monas	354907 4786687
Cabeza Tortorios	353694 4785749
Horcada Camburero	353914 4785511
Summit	353605 4784867
Fresnedal gully	354199 4785516

Bridge over the Urdon river - **WALK 2**

WALK NO. 14 - SOTRES TO ALIVA AND FUENTE DE

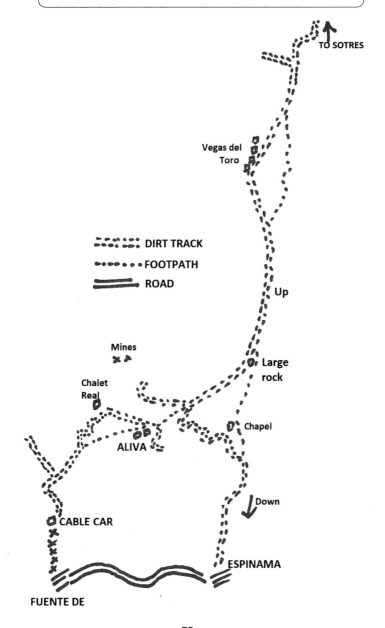

TO SOTRES

Vegas del Toro

DIRT TRACK
FOOTPATH
ROAD

Up

Mines

Chalet Real

Large rock

Chapel

ALIVA

Down

CABLE CAR

ESPINAMA

FUENTE DE

WALK NO. 14

SOTRES TO THE ALIVA REFUGE
AND THE FUENTE DÉ CABLE CAR

An easy walk, taking you to two of the landmarks of the Picos.

Distance	13 km linear
Ascent	1,100 metres
Overall grade	Easy
Terrain	Dirt tracks and footpaths
Exposure	Nil
Highest point	1,964 metres

Leave Sotres downhill on the road. At a sharp right-hand bend go straight ahead downhill on a dirt road. Pass above the huts of El Texu and where the track swings to the right to reach the huts keep straight on. Continue on the track for about 2.5 kilometres until the track swings right, some way before another group of cabins (the Vegas del Toro). At the bend there is a field wall on the left. A small footpath follows the left side of the wall, passing the Vegas del Toro at some distance. It rejoins the dirt road farther on. If you miss the field wall on the left just stay on the dirt track, but the path is more interesting.

- Once back on the dirt road, follow it uphill. You will pass through a gate and then pass by a small hut. At a junction of tracks (Point A) take the right fork. You will pass to the right of a huge isolated rock, which was dumped here by a glacier. The track leads along the top of a glacial moraine. You will soon see the green roof of the Aliva hotel/refuge ahead. At a three-way junction take the central route and go uphill all the way to Aliva, which has a restaurant and a bar, and is therefore a good place for a rest.

- From Aliva, continue up the track to the right of the hotel, passing the Chalet Real (an old hunting lodge) over to the right. The dirt road winds its way up the hill, but a footpath starts on the left, only 100 metres or so from Aliva. The path cuts out several bends. Otherwise you can simply follow the track upwards. It swings to the left and passes below high peaks on the right, before reaching a junction with a track coming in from the right. Take the left fork here. It soon swings left, and within a few minutes you will reach the top station of the Fuente Dé cable car, which you can descend in at the cost of a few euros. There is not much at the bottom, but it is a spectacular ride.

- If you prefer walking all the way to Fuente Dé instead of using the cable car, at Point A, just before the big rock, take the left fork and follow the track across a green valley. Pass a cattle shed and then a remote chapel. Join a major track, which descends in zigzags to eventually reach a road at the village of Espinama. From there a walk of about 3 kilometres up the road takes you to Fuente Dé. This is a popular walk, but the last time I did this there was no footpath between Espinama and Fuente Dé. The road was the only option. I have been informed (in 2017) that a new path has been opened, but at this time I cannot describe it.

A Parador Nacional and the Hotel Rebeca are situated near the foot of the cable car. There is not much to do apart from eat and drink, but Fuente Dé is a good base for starting out again next day (for example, see Walks 17 to 19). One way to return to Sotres, of course, is to take the *teleférico* and walk back via Aliva.

GPS REFERENCES (UTM)

Start	357963 4788082
Vegas del Toro	356415 4784903
Aliva hotel/refuge	354713 4781006
Cable car top	353179 4779477

Sotres from the peak of Cuetu Tejau – **WALK 6**

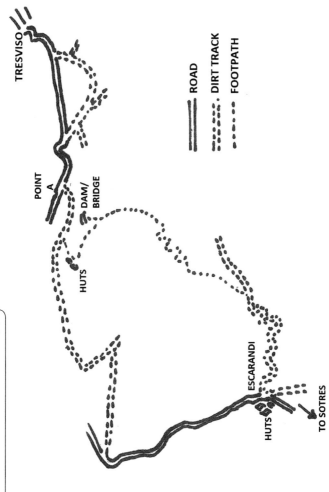

WALK NO. 15 - SOTRES TO TREVISO

TRESVISO

POINT A

DAM/BRIDGE

HUTS

ESCARANDI

HUTS

TO SOTRES

ROAD

DIRT TRACK

FOOTPATH

WALK NO. 15

SOTRES TO TRESVISO

An easy one-way walk, taking you to the isolated village of Tresviso via a remote valley route. This walk begins and ends at Escarandi, a car park some 3 km up the road from Sotres in the direction of Tresviso. Returning by the same route is necessary unless transport is arranged.

Distance	9 km linear (18 km return)
Ascent	250 metres out; 650 metres return
Overall grade	Easy
Terrain	Dirt tracks and footpaths
Exposure	Nil
Highest point	1,310 metres

- At the car park at Escarandi, two broad dirt tracks begin. Walk down the lower, left-hand track, signposted Vao de los Lobos, heading south-east. There are bends in the track. You can take shortcuts on some of them on cattle tracks. Stay on or near the main track for 1.5 kilometres (ignore a path going left after 1 km), until you have gone around some sharp bends and are in a broad green valley. At this point the track crosses a watercourse (dry at times). The track goes on to contour on the right-hand side of the valley above the watercourse, but leave the track at the watercourse and look for a route on the left side of the stream.

- The path is not easy to find at first. It generally follows the course of the stream, but keeps always to the left and does not descend as rapidly as the stream. But it follows the valley in a north-easterly direction. Look for cairns. Do not follow the very bottom by the stream, but look for the path a little higher. There are several cattle tracks, which can confuse the issue, but as you descend the valley there are cairns marking the true path, which in the lower part of the valley takes some big zigzags. At one point a minor path turns right and heads back up the valley, but ignore it and keep going in the same general direction. You should be following the line of the stream, which should be getting gradually further below you on your right.

Eventually the path swings to the left. You will have a great view ahead down the Urdón canyon, but the path goes above a tributary stream coming from the left. From here the path contours for a while. Ignore another path that goes to the right to a dam, which you can see below. Stay on the higher path, which becomes partly overgrown. You will reach a stream with some cabins on the other side. Cross the stream, and ascend a track to the right of the buildings. The track goes to the east and joins the Sotres/Tresviso road (Point A on the sketch map).

- Turn right to walk along the road for approximately 0.5 km. Go round a sharp bend and then take a track to the right, which continues to the east. Keep parallel to the road, but at a lower level. You will pass another track, which comes in from the right. Go past some huts and then, at a junction, take the left fork, which ascends to join the road once more by a footpath signpost. Turn right along the road, and after 200 metres you will enter the village.

In the village there is a large shelter with picnic tables, and near there you will find a bar.

- It is best to return to Escarandi by the outward route. When you pick up the track at Point A, stay on the main track and ignore one at a higher level. After about 1 km on the track take a left turn down to the cabins to cross the stream.

GPS REFERENCES (UTM)

Start	360442 4788588
Watercourse	361483 4788603
Along the path	362056 4789406
Swing left	362511 4790141
Cabins	362172 4790614
Track	363320 4790626
Tresviso	364604 4790740

The ridge below Picas del Jierru – **WALK 11**

WALK NO. 16 - VALDOMINGUERO

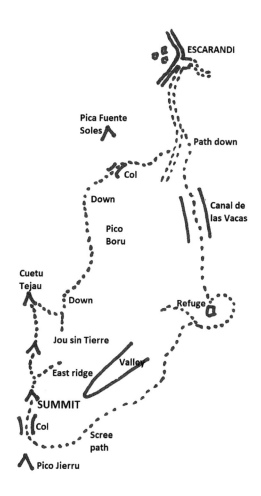

ESCARANDI

Pica Fuente
Soles

Path down

Col

Down

Canal de
las Vacas

Pico
Boru

Cuetu
Tejau

Down

Jou sin Tierre

Refuge

East ridge

Valley

SUMMIT

Col

Scree
path

Pico Jierru

WALK NO. 16

THE VALDOMINGUERO RIDGE

An excellent walk and scramble along high peaks way above the village of Sotres. Considerable exposure. Not suitable for anybody with vertigo.

Distance	15 km
Ascent	1,150 metres
Overall grade	Strenuous
Terrain	Footpaths and rock
Exposure	Exposed scrambling along a ridge
Highest point	2,265 metres

Much of this walk is the same as Walk 6, but this route is considerably more exciting and exposed.

Begin at el Jito de Escarandi, 3 km from Sotres.

• From the car park take the right-hand uphill track, which is signposted to the Andara refuge. Follow the track for 0.75 kilometres and then take a path downhill to the left. Go right at the bottom and cross a meadow. At the far end follow a footpath uphill to the left side of the valley bottom. The path is not difficult to find but if you lose it, follow the valley bottom straight on until you reach the Andara refuge. Face the refuge door and take a track to the left, but turn right uphill as soon as you can and zigzag upwards until you see the refuge below on your right. Continue upwards to reach a level area with a pond (often dry in summer and autumn) marked by a circle of stones. A number of paths head off in different directions from here.

- From the pond, take the path to the west, into a valley. After only a few metres, take the left fork where a red arrow points the way. The path ascends on the flanks of the hills to the left (south) side of the valley (the Pozo de Andara). Follow the path past disused mineshafts (these are numbered, and there are 100 of them altogether) as it gradually ascends. Keep right where the shafts are protected with green fencing.

- The path ascends to a col and then crosses a scree slope, with a valley full of chaotic rocks below on the right. But there is no difficulty on the well-defined scree path. After crossing another col the path continues upwards to the green Collado de Valdominguero, which separates Pico Jierru to the left from Valdominguero on the right. Turn right at the collado and ascend a steep hill, which appears impenetrable.

- The next section of the route is a scramble, not a walk. There is no official route. Take care along here, and follow the easiest route you can find, basically keeping as close as you safely can to the top of the ridge. The mountain has several summits, of which the highest (2,265 metres) is only 300 metres in distance from the col. However, it is not easy going and you must cross other tops to reach it.

- From the summit of Valdominguero, the scramble continues over subsidiary tops for a further distance of 250 metres. It doesn't sound much, but it is a continual scramble and not for the faint hearted. Although the rocky ridge is broad enough, there are significant drops to the sides. At the final top you will encounter a fixed sling, which indicates that using ropes is not out of the question (although we did it without).

It is an exciting route, with great views and a sense of accomplishment at the end of the ridge for ordinary walkers such as me.

- At the end of the scramble you will leave Valdominguero, but remain on high ground. Two subsidiary ridges now begin. Take the one to the left. This route stays high and follows the ridgeline to the north over several more summits, principally Picos del Jou sin Tierre (2,171 metres) and Cuetu Tejau (2,129 metres) from where there are great views straight down to the village of Sotres. On all this latter part of the ridge there is significant exposure to the left, but the right-hand slopes, while rocky, are gentle.

- So, from Valdominguero, simply keep left and to the high ground all the way to Cuetu Tejau, then descend to the east over rocky slabs as best you can, into a valley bottom, where you will find a good footpath coming down the valley from the right. Turn left along it, and follow it to the left side of a hill ahead (Pico Boru), and then, still staying high, and avoiding any temptation to go sharp downhill to the left, the path leads you with cairns downhill in a northerly direction.

- When you descend to a grassy col, with the peak of Pica Fuente Soles in front of you, turn right and descend to the dirt track from the Andara refuge, where a left turn will take you back to Escarandi.

GPS REFERENCES (UTM)

Start	360439 4788579
Andara refuge	360904 4786019
Pond	360913 4785802
Along the path	359461 4784292
Valdominguero col	358856 4784447
Summit	359008 4784703
Cuetu Tejau	358919 4785832
Don't go left	359367 4786135
Grassy col	359721 4787342

WALK NO. 17 - FUENTE DE TO HORCADOS ROJOS

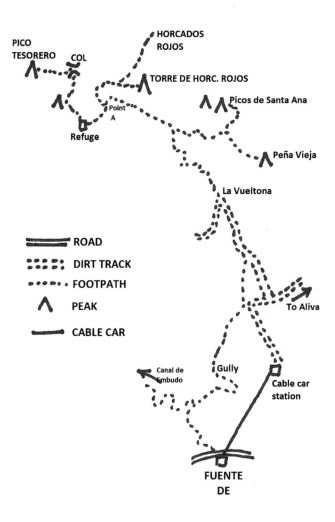

ROAD

DIRT TRACK

FOOTPATH

PEAK

CABLE CAR

WALK NO. 17

FUENTE DÉ CABLE CAR TO TORRE DE HORCADOS ROJOS

A high-level walk to a peak above the Verónica refuge. Other nearby peaks can also be accessed from this route.

Distance	11 km
Ascent	1,070 metres approx.
Overall grade	Moderate
Terrain	Footpaths, boulders and shale
Exposure	There are two tops. The route to the second and main summit is somewhat exposed.
Highest point	2,568 metres

Alternatives along the same general route are to ascend Pico Tesorero, Picos de Santa Ana (serious exposure at the summit) or Peña Vieja. The sketch map shows their location. The Picos de Santa Ana have two peaks, the highest being the western one, for which you should circuit to the north of the eastern peak.

- From Fuente Dé take the cable car to El Cable, the top station, at 1,800 metres above sea level. Take the broad dirt track from the station in a northerly direction for about 1 kilometre. The track veers to the right. Then take the next track to the left, heading north-west. After a further 1.25 km you will reach La Vueltona, where the main track swings sharply to the left. Do not turn left but go straight ahead, on a path. This well-marked path takes you steadily uphill, zigzagging across rocky ground. Ignore any paths going up to the right (unless you are taking the Santa Ana or Peña Vieja alternatives) and stay on the main path. *In the spring, and until late*

June, parts of this path are covered in snow and great care is required when crossing them. A fall would be dangerous.

- As you ascend, eventually you will see the silver Cabaña Verónica ahead and above. It is a small refuge made from the gun turret of an aircraft carrier. Before you reach the refuge, there is a junction of paths (Point A on the sketch map). The right fork takes you to Horcados Rojos. The left turn takes you to the refuge and on to Pico Tesorero.

- **For the Torre de Horcados Rojos**, take the right fork at Point A and go uphill over rocky ground, to the edge of a precipice, with views down into the Jou de los Boches below, and of the Naranjo farther on. Torre de Horcados Rojos is the peak above to your right. To reach it, turn right at the top of the precipice, and walk up a steep, shaly path, which is loose at times. There are two tops. The first is easy. For the second, higher peak you must scramble across a short narrow ridge. A fair head for heights is necessary, and take care.

- Descend the way you came, and on the way back it is good to make a diversion to the Verónica refuge, where coffee, soup, beers and so on normally await you in summer and autumn. On leaving the refuge, return to El Cable by the outward route.

- For Pico Tesorero, from Point A continue on the path to the refuge and then behind the refuge go north, over rocky ground, and follow the broad ridgeline . Keep a weather station to your left. Pico Tesorero is ahead, a pyramid-shaped peak. Continue over the rocks towards Tesorero, and keep to the right below the first hill ahead of you. Ascend to the col below the right-hand side of the peak, and from there turn left to walk/scramble 100 metres steeply up to reach the summit. It is not technically difficult, but involves some exposure and requires a head for heights.

- For Santa Ana or Peña Vieja, on the main path from La Vueltona, take the next path to the right to ascend a gully called La Canalona. The loose path zigzags up the gully. At the top turn left for Santa Ana, or right for Peña Vieja. The former is very exposed at the summit. To reach it you should circuit round the right-hand side of the summit and approach it from behind. For Peña Vieja the path is clear, following the contour to the right before taking a zigzag route marked by cairns to the top.

NOTE

For extra excitement for strong walkers, instead of using the cable car you can ascend from Fuente Dé on foot by a spectacular route. This makes for a very strenuous day. From the foot of the cable car, cross the road and go to the left across the field used as an overflow car park. A path leads to the Canal del Embudo, the massive gully going up to the west. Follow this path, but at a junction before starting the ascent of the gully, take the right fork. It leads up to the cliffs to the left of the cable car's trajectory. After reaching a level area above a waterfall, go to the left, where a path enters a narrow gully and ascends steeply. At one point you will reach a rock which would be impassable, but a fixed rope enables you to pull yourself up and gain the higher reaches. The route continues upwards, sometimes almost vertically, and at the top enters a delightful limestone valley. At the far end of the valley head to the right across open moor to reach the top cable car station, or a path takes you on a shortcut to the north-east to join the track near La Vueltona.

GPS REFERENCES (UTM)

Start	352649 4778418
Top of cable car	353210 4779450
La Vueltona	352441 4781185
Verónica refuge	350866 4782046
Torre de Horcados Rojos	351262 4782334
Pico Tesorero	350384 4782528

Alternative ascent:	
Right fork	352348 4779024
Go left	352760 4779295
Into the Jenduda gully	352450 4779457
Top of gully	352598 4779939

On the Valdominguero ridge – **WALK 16**

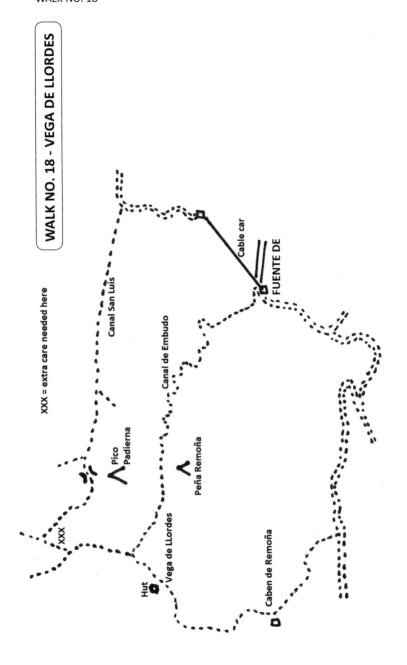

WALK NO. 18 - VEGA DE LLORDES

XXX = extra care needed here

Canal San Luis

Canal de Embudo

Cable car

FUENTE DE

Pico Padierna

Peña Remoña

XXX

Vega de LLordes

Hut

Caben de Remoña

WALK NO. 18

FUENTE DÉ TO VEGA DE LLORDES

A route from Fuente Dé, via the cable car, to the magnificent Vega de Llordes, a high-level glacial meadow surrounded by limestone peaks.

Distance	11 km or 13 km
Ascent	1,070 metres either way
Overall grade	Strenuous
Terrain	Footpaths, boulders and shale
Exposure	Reasonable head for heights needed.
Highest point	2,250 metres

The alternative route avoids the cable car, and is a walk of 13 km. The ascent is 1,070 metres, and is strenuous.

The Vega de Llordes is a high-level meadow, with a glacial moraine at one end. It is surrounded by high peaks such as Pico Padierna and Peña Remoña. A stream flows across the meadow to disappear into a cave.

Via the cable car and Canal San Luis:

This route is dangerous in mist or when the ground is covered in snow. But when the going is clear it is excellent. Do not attempt it in poor conditions.

- Take the cable car to the top station, and walk on the main track for just less than 1 kilometre to a point where the track bends sharply to the right. Leave the track here and turn sharp left on a footpath. You should see the path ahead. It keeps to the left (south) side of the valley ahead, going west.

- The valley is the Canal de San Luis. The path takes a gradual ascent. At a junction of paths, a painted sign

93

indicates that the right turn is correct for Llordes. In fact, you can go either way. The right turn is slightly longer, but is a better-quality path, while the left turn leads you to a line of cairns ascending over difficult rocky terrain. The object is to reach the Collado de las Nieves (the Snowy Col). Take the right fork, and follow cairns until the path starts to head to the right towards a major depression (the Hoyo Oscuro). Then leave the path and go left to ascend a green gully to reach the Collado de la Nieves, where the ground levels out.

- A short walk up to the left from the collado takes you to the spectacular summit of Pico Padierna (2,314 metres). It is well worth the effort. Take a deep breath before stepping on to the platform at the summit. Take care, as the far side is a precipice.

- You will see the meadows of Vega de Llordes below the peak to the south-west. Return to the Collado de las Nieves, from where you **MUST** follow the cairns all the way down to the vega. To go directly would be seriously dangerous. The cairns follow a meandering route over difficult ground. The tendency is slightly north of west. Take great care to follow the cairns over wild limestone country, and avoid any potholes. Continue following the cairns, and do not be in a hurry to descend to the left. Eventually a path comes up from the left, clearly marked with cairns. Take this path downhill, going diagonally down the cliff face. *It may not suit those with vertigo*.

- At the foot of the cliff, a path goes to the right, but instead turn left across grassy land and descend to the vega. At the far (western) end of the vega you will see a cabin. Near there is where the stream disappears into a cave. It makes a good destination for the walk.

- From the cabin in the vega, walk back across the vega to the east, keeping close to the left (northern) side of the meadow. You will soon reach a path that ascends to cross a glacial moraine, which is riddled with old mineshafts. Make for a path that is immediately below Pico Padierna, as far to the left side of the vega as possible. Once it has crossed the moraine, the path starts a twisting descent towards Fuente Dé, which you will soon see below.

- The descent is via the Canal de Embudo. The initial view is daunting, with precipices in the gully, but the path never reaches them. The difficulty comes from the length of continual descent and the shaly ground, which can be slippery. Walking poles are a distinct advantage. A long descent of over 1,000 metres takes you back to the bottom station of the cable car.

ALTERNATIVE ROUTE

- Exiting the car park at the foot of the cable car, turn left along the road and follow it round some bends as it becomes a broad dirt track. Follow the track for about 2 kilometres and, at a junction, turn right on the track going uphill. It becomes steep at times. Walk on this track for about 2 km from the junction, and then leave the track and turn right to walk uphill across grassy slopes to reach a hut (the Caben de Remoña).

- From here, go straight uphill towards a huge gully to the north-west of the cabin. A loose, stony footpath goes into the gully (the Canal de Pedabejo) and it takes a zigzag route across the scree-filled floor of the gully. It is steep and loose, but it is a well-trodden and cairned path. Continue to the very top of the gully and, where it levels out into a small valley, take the path at the far right-hand corner of the valley to reach a pass at Alto de la Canal.

- From here descend on a good path into the Vega de Llordes. Ignore a path going off to the left as you descend.

- At the foot of the incline, in the magnificent Vega de Llordes, you will reach the cabin referred to in the walk described above. From there you should follow the same directions as above to return to Fuente Dé.

GPS REFERENCES (UTM)

Top of cable car	353210 4779450
Start of path left	352883 4780164
Collado de las Nieves	350735 4780008
Pico Padierna summit	350774 4779825
Path down (approximate)	349734 4780255
Cabin in the vega	349608 4779344
Top of Canal del Embudo	351097 4779444

Alternative ascent:	
Start	352649 4778418
Right turn	351628 4777346
Leave the track (approx.)	350374 4777521
Canal de Pedabejo	349633 4778363
Alto de la Canal	349522 4778761

WALK NO. 19 - PICOS DE CAMARA

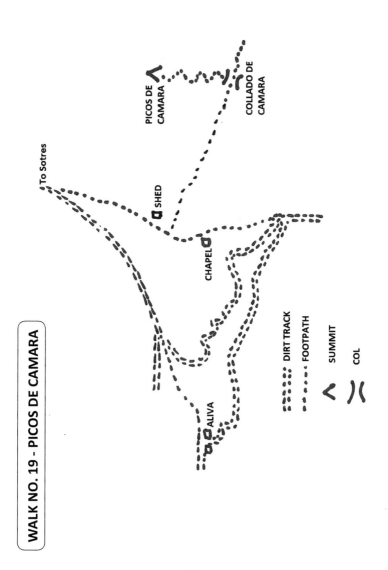

PICOS DE CAMARA

COLLADO DE CAMARA

To Sotres

SHED

CHAPEL

ALIVA

DIRT TRACK

FOOTPATH

SUMMIT

COL

WALK NO. 19

ALIVA REFUGE TO THE PICOS DE CÁMARA

An opportunity to bag a relatively easy but spectacular peak in the Eastern massif.

Distance	**12 km (6 km each way)**
Ascent	**630 metres**
Overall grade	**Moderate**
Terrain	**Footpaths, boulders and scree**
Exposure	**None, but a danger of rolling rocks.**
Highest point	**2,100 metres**

On leaving the Aliva hotel/refuge take the track to the south, which quickly swings to the east, and follow it to reach Campomenor, a grassy area just to the south of the chapel of la Virgen de las Nieves (the Virgin of the Snows). You will see the chapel from above as you descend from Aliva, in a delightful meadowland setting. On the way you can take shortcuts and avoid the bends in the track by walking across green cattle pasture.

- To the north of the chapel, in the same meadows, there is a cattle shed. Between the chapel and the shed take a broad and somewhat eroded path, which ascends the hills to the east. It follows a line of pylons, broadly speaking. The path goes north-east and then east up easy ground to reach the col Collado de Cámara at 1,706 metres altitude. At this point the path goes through a gate and descends the eastern slopes. But, instead of following it through the gate, turn left and ascend the nose of the hill, now going north. You will need to cross a wall, and the ground becomes a rough scree slope, becoming looser and rougher as you ascend. Take care with falling rocks. Otherwise the ascent, continuing in a northerly direction, is without complication, and leads you to the first summit of the Picos de Cámara.

- Apart from the loose boulders the ascent is just moderate, but once on the sharp summit you will find yourself in high mountain country, and the views of several neighbouring peaks are spectacular.

The nearby peaks may also be accessible, but I have not yet explored them. Pico Cortes is the highest of these, but is accessible from Aliva by another route which ascends from the valley 1 km north of the chapel. The first summit of the Cámara peaks is rewarding enough for a moderate walk, and you can return to Aliva or walk north on the main track through the Duje valley north to Sotres.

GPS REFERENCES (UTM)

Aliva	354713 4781006
South of the chapel	356281 4780760
Collado de Cámara	357592 4780851
Picos de Cámara	357728 4781607

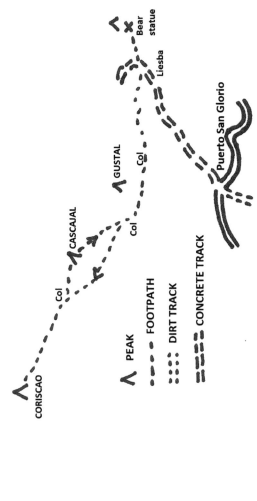

WALK NO. 20 - CORISCAO

CORISCAO

Col

CASCAJAL

Col

GUSTAL

Col

Col

Liesba

Bear
statue

Puerto San Glorio

PEAK

FOOTPATH

DIRT TRACK

CONCRETE TRACK

WALK NO. 20

CORISCAO

The ascent of a high peak on the edge of the national park.

Distance	13 km
Ascent	800 metres
Overall grade	Easy
Terrain	Good footpaths
Exposure	None
Highest point	2,223 metres

Coriscao is an outlying peak on the very southern edge of the Picos de Europa. Along this route you will encounter Parque Nacional signposts on the park boundary. The walk is easy, with plenty of interest and great views to the Central and Eastern massifs.

Begin at Puerto San Glorio, 19 km from the Vega de Liébana, near Potes. From Potes take the N621 road towards Riaño. The road winds up and up, in a seemingly never-ending way, until the San Glorio pass, where you can park at the left side of the main road. If you wish you can turn right here and drive up a recently concreted track to the Liesba col, where you can also park. This shortens the walk, but from the main road the walk is a pleasant stroll up the track with little traffic.

- From San Glorio walk north-east up the concrete track. After less than 2 kilometres you will reach the Liesba col, at 1,700 metres elevation, close to where a huge concrete bear marks a viewpoint and says something about the local wildlife. (You are not likely to see a real bear.)

- Once you arrive at the col, turn left. Ascend in a westerly direction on a grassy hill before the path goes down to a col that separates this green hill from the next hill, Peña del Gustal, which has a rocky and inaccessible aspect.

- Don't attempt to climb it, but keep left and cross horizontally to the south of Gustal to reach another col on the far side. Continue on the same hillside to pass below the next peak (Peña Cascajal), and you will reach a broad col separating Cascajal from Coriscao. All you have to do now is ascend the hillside to reach the summit.

- The approach to the summit is interesting, with rocky crags falling away on the right-hand side to the valley below. The walk is without difficulties, apart from the steady ascent up the final pyramid.

- The view north from the summit is of the Central and Eastern massifs. To the south and west are other hills of the Cordillera Cantábrica, which are outside the national park limits.

- From the summit, you can return largely by the same route. However, for variety stay high and traverse the top of the hill of Cascajal, at the far end of which a decent footpath descends to the east and joins up once more with the main footpath.

- Once you have rejoined the main path beyond Cascajal there are few options. Stay on the main path and reverse the outward route back to Puerto San Glorio.

GPS REFERENCES (UTM)

Puerto San Glorio	356263 4769763
Liesba Col	357574 4770792
Coriscao summit	353984 4771969

WALK NO. 21 - POSADA TO CORONA

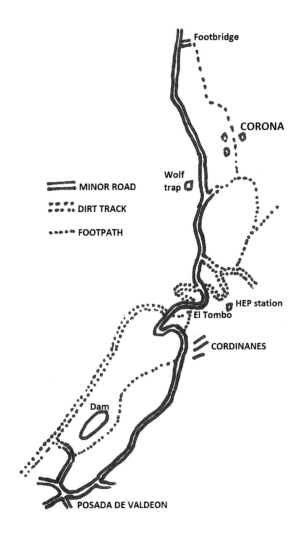

WALK NO. 21

POSADA DE VALDEÓN TO CORONA CIRCUIT

A delightful valley walk, with options providing longer and shorter routes. The main walk is a figure-of-eight route, so it can be shortened by 50 per cent.

Distance	14 km
Ascent	650 metres
Overall grade	Moderate
Terrain	Good footpaths and tracks
Exposure	None
Highest point	936 metres

- In Posada de Valdeón, with your back to the front door of the Hostal Corona, go left, pass a doctor's surgery and take the next street right. Turn right on the next street, and at the following junction take a left turn, which leads down past some fields and reaches a bridge over the river. Turn right on a path just before the bridge. It can be a quagmire, so walk in the field to its left for a few metres and then step back across to the path. It leads to an *area recreativa* (a picnic site). To the right of this, a track leads on to skirt the right bank of a lovely reservoir. Pass close to the dam at the far end of the lake and keep going along a grassy terrace. Then cross a meadow to reach the road from Posada to Cain.

- Turn left to walk down the road and through the village of Cordiñanes. At the very bottom of the hill, turn right immediately before the road crosses a bridge and follow a track to join the road again (the road has made a big loop). Across the road you will find the viewpoint the Mirador of El Tombo, with a statue of a rebeco deer, and a relief map showing the names of the neighbouring peaks of the Central massif.

- Take a dirt track going downhill to the left of the road. The track descends to the left, then swings right to cross to the far side of the road. Continue on the track to the floor of the valley. You will pass a fence where a new (2017) via ferrata begins. Ignore it – this book is about walking. Continue on the track. Turn right at a junction and cross a bridge. You will pass a hydroelectric building and a medieval burial ground over to the right. Stay on the main track, which starts to ascend to the right, but just after a right-hand bend, and next to a *fuente*, take a footpath going uphill to the left (north).

- The path rises gradually, above a line of pylons. At one point there is a right fork, which is a dead end, so take the left fork. It leads you past the highest of the pylons, and then down and to the left into a valley, passing an old but refurbished hut to arrive at a track near the river.

- Turn right along the track and you will reach a lovely meadow with the chapel of Corona on the right and several huts. (*Corona is known in legend as the place where Menendez Pelayo was crowned king of Spain in the ninth century or thereabouts, after defeating the Moors in battle. 'Corona' means 'crown'.*)

- From Corona continue downhill and to the north, crossing meadows, and then along a path to the right signposted for Cain. The path soon descends again. Go downhill to reach a track near the riverbank. Turn right along it until 1.25 km from Corona a footbridge leads you to the other side of the stream and the road. This point is called Las Vegas. (It is a bit different from the one in Nevada!) Turn left and walk up the road. There is very little traffic on it here. It leads you to the Chorco de los Lobos, the Wolf Trap, (literally) where an information board explains, in Spanish, of course, how they used to trap and kill the wolves, which were a menace to livestock.

- From the Wolf Trap continue up the road to return to the El Tombo viewpoint. You will pass a *fuente* with nice cold water on the way.

- From the El Tombo viewpoint, cross the road and take a signposted path that swings to the right to cross the road yet again at a higher level and then goes uphill, passing a fenced area with beehives on the right. The track swings left, and then goes more or less along the contour with the river below to the left. Follow the track without deviation to pass the reservoir to your left. At the far end of the reservoir do not cross the bridge, but take a fork to the right to follow another track that takes you to a bridge at the far (southern) edge of Posada de Valdeón. Turn left and cross the bridge to return to the start.

EASY OPTION

For the shorter version of the walk, follow the above route as far as the El Tombo viewpoint. Then turn around, cross the road and follow the signposted path as described above. Return to Posada on the track indicated in the above description.

GPS REFERENCES (UTM)

Posada de Valdeón	344040 4779488
Mirador del Tombo	345352 4781624
Path to the left	345483 4782080
Corona	345383 4782957
Footbridge	345084 4784180
Wolf trap	345306 4782809
On the track to Posada	344872 4781489

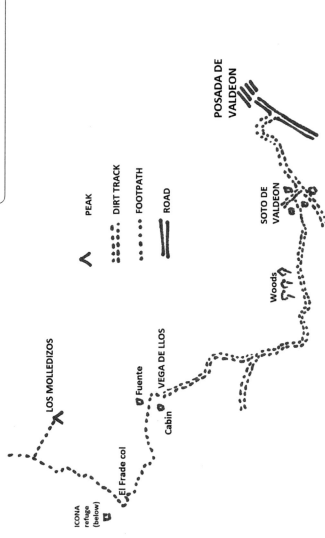

WALK NO. 22 - LOS MOLLEDIZOS

PEAK

DIRT TRACK

FOOTPATH

ROAD

POSADA DE VALDEON

SOTO DE VALDEON

Woods

LOS MOLLEDIZOS

Fuente

VEGA DE LLOS

Cabin

El Frade col

ICONA refuge (below)

WALK NO. 22

POSADA DE VALDEÓN
TO THE PEAK OF LOS MOLEDIZOS

An ascent to a peak overlooking the Valdeón valley from the Western massif.

Distance	18 km
Ascent	1,440 metres
Overall grade	Strenuous
Terrain	Good footpaths and tracks
Exposure	Minimal
Highest point	2,256 metres

You may start in Posada de Valdeón, although taking a four-wheel drive to Vega de Llos saves 700 metres of ascent, making a strenuous route into a moderate one.

From Posada to Vega de Llos the walk is 5 km (one way). The ascent is 700 metres.

From Vega de Llos to the summit the walk is 4 km (one way). The ascent is 740 metres.

To walk from Posada, take the road towards Soto de Valdeón but turn right on a dirt road just beyond the Hotel Picos de Europa. Follow the track to Soto de Valdeón and then turn right on a street between some houses. After about 100 metres, go left on a sloping path across the bottom of a hill. The path ascends a gradual incline, and soon you will enter woods. At any turn-offs keep to the right and stay on the main track. When you meet a dirt road at a T-junction, by a *fuente* at Collado Bustiello, turn right and follow it uphill to the Vega de Llos, an open meadow area with a hut. Continue beyond the hut to another *fuente*.

- From the *fuente*, take a path to the north-west, aiming for the col of El Frade ahead and above. There are cattle tracks, but one stands out as a footpath. You should be ascending generally north-west, with high mountains above to your right. The paths cross grassy slopes and circuit the head of some watercourses until finally a steeper ascent via a green gully leads you to the col.

- Go through a cleft in the ridge, from where you will see down towards Vegabaño and the unmanned ICONA refuge on the northern side. Turn right here along a broad ridge.

- Follow the ridge uphill. The path becomes shaly as it takes a zigzag route up towards the Western massif. You will reach a shoulder where a rough scree slope goes ahead across the western slopes of Los Moledizos. The path crosses the sparse scree, and then leads you steeply up a gully, the Canal del Perro (the Dog's Gully). There is no real exposure here, but it may be a little airy for those not accustomed to heights. At the top of the gully you will reach the Collado del Burro (the Donkey's Col). The going gets easier, and the path will lead you northwards. If you kept going you would reach Vega Huerta, a crossroads of paths in the high hills. To ascend the peak of Los Moledizos, once the ground has levelled you can ascend off-piste in a south-easterly direction to reach the summit.

The easiest option is to return by the outward route. To make it a circular route you can continue on to Vega Huerta and then descend the enormous Capozo gully to return to Posada. That is a big day, and I do not describe this route here. However, you will be able to navigate the route with the aid of the recommended Adrados maps.

GPS REFERENCES (UTM)

Posada de Valdeón	344040 4779488
Vega de Llos	340855 4780822
Collado del Frade	339789 4781275
Collado del Burro	340464 4782398
Los Moledizos summit	340782 4781900
Vega Huerta	340695 4783964
Path down Capozo gully	341491 4784338
Near the bottom	343388 4783944

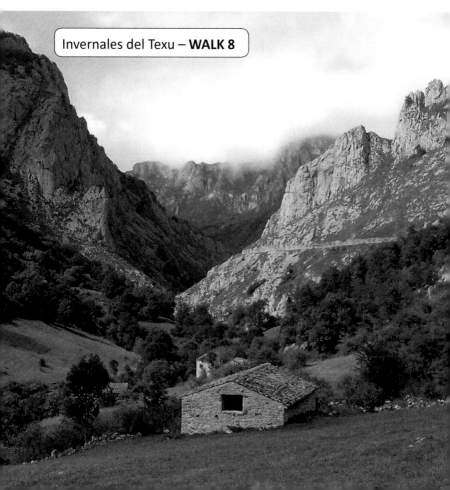

Invernales del Texu – **WALK 8**

WALK NO. 23 - TORRE BERMEJA

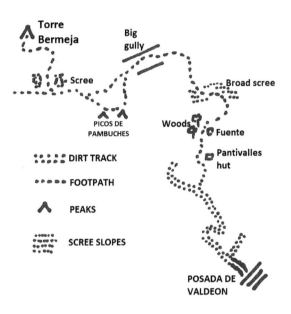

Torre Bermeja

Big gully

Scree

PICOS DE PAMBUCHES

Broad scree

Woods

Fuente

Pantivalles hut

POSADA DE VALDEON

⦂⦂⦂⦂ DIRT TRACK

●●●●● FOOTPATH

⋀ PEAKS

⦂⦂⦂ SCREE SLOPES

WALK NO. 23

POSADA DE VALDEÓN TO THE PEAK OF TORRE BERMEJA

An ascent of a major peak in the Western massif directly from the village of Posada de Valdeón.

Distance	14 km
Ascent	1,500 metres
Overall grade	Strenuous
Terrain	Footpaths, boulders and scree
Exposure	None
Highest point	2,400 metres

DO NOT ATTEMPT THIS WALK IN MIST. TAKE CARE TO NAVIGATE YOUR WAY BACK FROM THE SUMMIT.

- In Posada, walk down the street past the Hostal Abascal and cross a bridge. At the far side, go slightly left and take a track uphill. Ignore an immediate turn into a field on the left. The track swings right, climbing steadily across terraced fields and passing farm buildings. After about 1 kilometre uphill on the track, at a cairn, take a footpath to the right, and continue uphill. The path leads you to a shoulder of the hill where, to your right, you should see the Pantivalles hut at 1,249 metres altitude.

- The path keeps over to the left of the hut, goes straight across the shoulder of the hill, descends slightly and continues on the right flank of the next hillside. Then swing left and uphill once more. Soon you will reach a *fuente* on the edge of woods, after which the path goes out to the right and into open ground, where a vague path heads uphill crossing the lower parts of a scree.

- The route is marked by cairns, but the path continually divides, so take the easiest option at any time. (I find it best to make a broad sweep to the right side of the scree and then cross back to the left.) Continue up towards the high mountains. As you ascend straight towards a narrow gully with a steeper scree, do not despair. Before you get there, behind the first bank of rocks on the left, the Pambuches gully ascends to the west. Follow this route, which goes uphill on a cairned path and, at times, over boulder fields.

- Ascend the gully until, climbing steeply, you reach a green col, the Collado de Pambuches, at almost 2,000 metres. Cross over the col and enter another depression, with scree slopes over to the right. Keep to the path, which is over to the left as you ascend. There is a cave in the rocks over on the right, the Hoyo del Bufon. Beyond it a smaller gully, the Canal del Bufon, goes steeply up to the right. Do not go straight on, but take this route to the right. At first it is a scramble up loose scree.

- At the top of this slope you will find more open ground. Follow the path, which eventually swings to the left towards the summit ridge. To reach the top, follow it to the left of the summit and then swing right to gain the topmost point at 2,400 metres.

- ***Take great care to return by the same route. As you descend from the peak it is easy to go straight down the hill, but the path goes to the left and then swings right again to reach the Canal del Bufon***. It would be dangerous to lose the correct route.

Turn left to descend the Pambuches gully again. But when you reach the Collado de Pambuches, instead of going straight down the hill, traverse across to the right, where you can easily access the Picos de Pambuches, which provide a great resting place with wonderful views directly down on to the village of Posada de Valdeón.

- From there, return to the gully and descend it, struggle across the scree to the right, make your way to the very welcome *fuente* for cold water, go down to the Pantivalles hut and back down the path and the track to Posada.

GPS REFERENCES (UTM)

Posada de Valdeón	344040 4779488
Path up	343473 4780336
Pantivalles hut	343536 4780761
Fuente	343392 4781271
Base of Pambuches gully	343108 4781748
Picos de Pambuches	342654 4781257
Canal del Bufon	341846 4781365
Torre Bermeja summit	341430 4781874

WALK NO. 24 - COLLADO JERMOSO

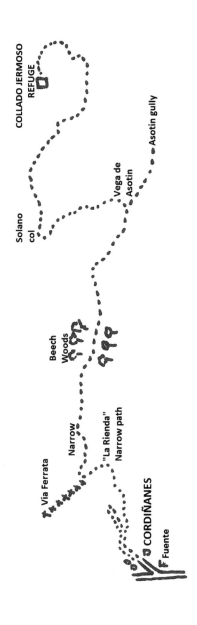

COLLADO JERMOSO
REFUGE

Solano
col

Vega de
Asotin

Asotin gully

Beech
Woods

Narrow

"La Rienda"
Narrow path

Via Ferrata

CORDIÑANES

Fuente

WALK NO. 24

CORDIÑANES TO
THE COLLADO JERMOSO REFUGE

A big and continual ascent to an amazing high mountain refuge perched above a cliff.

The distance is not great, so this can be done by strong walkers as an out-and-back walk within the day. But the ascent is significant, and there is some easy scrambling en route.

Distance	9 km one way
Ascent	1,400 metres
Overall grade	Strenuous
Terrain	Footpaths, boulders and scree
Exposure	Narrow sections of path above a vertical drop.
Highest point	2,047 metres

Begin the walk at the village of Cordiñanes, 3 kilometres from Posada de Valdeón. There is a *fuente* by the road at the top of the village, with parking for a few cars. From the *fuente*, walk along a street going north, to the right of the main road and through some houses. Keep going in the same direction until you pass the last house. Beyond this a broad track, marked with yellow and white paint, heads out into open country and goes north-east. After only 200 metres a path, with the yellow and white marks, goes to the right. Take this path uphill.

• The path crosses somewhat rocky ground, and soon starts a steeper ascent, taking zigzags and swinging north, to cross a narrow section above a precipice. This well-known path is known as La Rienda. It has recently been improved (2015–16) and is not difficult going. A fixed rope has been installed as a handrail, although experienced hill walkers may not need it. However, ***this section will not suit those with vertigo***.

• Having passed the precipice, the path ascends to a grassy ridge, from where a via ferrata goes downhill to the left. However, for this walk, ignore that and turn right to follow the path to the east. It crosses one or two more short but slightly exposed sections (with no rope to help you now), and then continues into beech woods (the Hayedo de Asotin). Cairns lead you diagonally through the woods, and gradually uphill. After you emerge at the far side of the woods, continue uphill on the left side of a broad valley.

• The path now takes a steeper line, going in zigzags, and reaches the open meadows of the Vega de Asotin. At the vega you will see the huge Asotin gully ahead, going up to the south-east. But our route goes to the left (north). Near the centre of the vega is a signpost pointing left for Collado Jermoso. Take this path to the north. It once more zigzags to reach a col at Collado Solano.

• The path now swings right, keeping to the right below the crest of the hill. Follow it as it ascends gradually. It then takes a downhill section for a distance of about half a kilometre, before swinging left into a broad valley. It now ascends steeply, across rocky ground.

• From here the walk becomes a scramble over rocky steps and boulders, and you may find yourself sometimes slithering across damp sections of rocky path. However, the route is clear, and although sometimes there are options en route, all the deviations should lead you to the same point. So take the line of least resistance. You are at this point very close to the refuge, but it does not come into view until you are very nearby. When you do see it, it will be a relief after your hard work. As you reach the highest parts of the walk/scramble you will see that the refuge is situated on a promontory above to your left.

The refuge is manned through the summer and into the early autumn. During that period you can buy lunch and drinks, and there is drinking water (untreated) from a tap outside the building. You are surrounded by high mountain views.

If you stay the night here, the next day you have two main options. Either:

(i) Cross las Colladinas to reach the Vega de Llordes, and descend to Fuente Dé (see Walk 18); or

(ii) Ascend to Tiro Callejo to scale one of the difficult high peaks above.

Otherwise, return to Cordiñanes by the outward route.

GPS REFERENCES (UTM)

Cordiñanes	345246 4781091
Path up	345500 4781291
Grassy ridge	345820 4781501
Vega de Asotin	347321 4781284
Collado Solano	347160 4781710
Collado Jermoso	348087 4781718

WALK NO. 25 - PEÑA REMOÑA

WALK NO. 25

PEÑA REMOÑA PEAK

An ascent to one of the peaks above the Vega de Llordes. The final ascent is easy enough, being mainly up grassy slopes, but the views from the summit are spectacular.

Distance	9.5 km each way
Ascent	1,100 metres
Overall grade	Strenuous
Terrain	Footpaths, boulders and scree
Exposure	A short, easy scramble on rocks.
Highest point	2,242 metres

Take the road from Posada de Valdeón to the south via Santa Marina. Continue, and pass above the village to reach a point where the road begins to descend and there is parking on each side of the road. This is the Puerto de Pandetrave.

- From Pandetrave a dirt track goes east and then north towards the Central massif. There are 4.5 kilometres of easy walking on the track (ignore a right turn towards Fuente Dé after about 3 km) to reach an open area (at Collado de Remoña) that is used as a car park. *If you have a car that you are happy to drive along a dirt track you could drive this part of the route, saving 4.5 km each way of walking. But bear in mind that the track is rough, and a hire car may not be insured for off-road use.* So, for this guide I can only say that you need to reach the parking area on foot (Point A on my sketch map). It is an easy walk, and on your return it gives you some options, described below.

- At Point A you will find various tracks, with signposts. While facing north, take the track uphill to the left,

120

signposted to Collado Jermoso. After a few metres the track swings right. Ignore another track going up to the left. The correct track is marked with yellow and white paint at times. Walk on towards the spectacular mountains ahead. The track becomes a footpath. You will soon reach a wooden animal corral on the left, with a *fuente* (the Pedabejo spring) beyond and below to the right. You now have two choices (at Point B on my sketch map).

- Your first option at Point B is to go straight on, at first on the level, then losing 50 metres of height, to reach the foot of the massive Pedabejo gully. Follow the path to the left up a short section on loose shale, and into the gully. It looks fierce, but the worst part is the first. The path crosses to the far side of the gully and then takes a zigzag route to the top. The quality of the path is very poor to begin with, but it improves as you go. Continue uphill with the enormous face of Torre Pedabejo on your right, to reach a level meadow at Alto de la Canal.

- The alternative at Point B is shorter, steeper and a little more exposed, and involves a short, easy scramble. With the *fuente* below to your right, look for a cairn to the left and from there follow a minor path going diagonally towards the cliff face. When you reach the cliffs there is a scramble with good holds on the rocks. Keep well over to the right on the rocks. The path resumes at the top. Continue to ascend, with a drop to the right, but it is a good broad path with no other dangers. It will bring you up to meet the main path at Alto de la Canal.

- The two paths meet in a small meadow. After going into the meadow, take a path to the right to ascend a further 20 metres until you begin to descend. On the right here a rocky outcrop provides great views of the Vega de Llordes (a glaciated meadow) below, of Pico Padierna ahead, of Peña Remoña to the far right, and of the Torre de Salinas to the left, as well as of many other spectacular limestone peaks. A truly wonderful spot.

- Return to the path and follow it downhill, going north-west. Ignore a left fork (signposted to Collado Jermoso). Continue all the way down to the vega, where you will find a cabin, and below it a stream which vanishes into a cave. The route from here is straight across the green vega, going east. You will cross the stream occasionally, and will be aiming for the rocky outcrops at the far end of the meadow. Peña Remoña is at the very far end of the line of peaks on the right. On reaching the rocky outcrops at the far end of the vega, start to ascend to the right and look for cairns which will lead you to the summit. If you do not find the cairns, simply make your way up the grassy slopes to the south-east, to reach the limestone ridge. Ensure that you keep across to the left, so that you reach the top and not the smaller summits to the right.

- The summit of Remoña has two peaks, both spectacular. The right-hand one is the higher, although this is not entirely obvious. At the top you will have great views above the Embudo gully, which descends to Fuente Dé. Pico Padierna is the peak facing you to the north, and you can see many peaks of the Central massif. The top station of the cable car is visible below to the east.

- Retrace your steps from the summit. Try to follow the cairns on the way back, and do not be in a hurry to descend too soon.

On the return there are options, described below. If you left your vehicle at Pandetrave you need to return there, obviously. But if you got there by taxi, you could descend on foot direct to Posada de Valdeón. Finally, if you left a car at Point A you will have time to ascend another peak, and I would suggest Pico Padierna.

- OPTION ONE: To return to Pandetrave retrace your steps across the vega and past the cabin. Ascend to Alto de la Canal, from where you can descend the Pedabejo gully. Continue on the path at the foot of the gully as it goes to the right, ignore a path going downhill to the left, follow the path back to Point B and then to Point A and then follow the track back to Pandetrave. This is 19 km in total for the day.

- OPTION TWO: **Do not take this option without a 1:25,000 map**. To return on foot to Posada de Valdeón, follow the directions for Option One as far as Point A, but do not take the dirt road to Pandetrave. Instead take a path downhill into a gully to the south-west. Cross the gully and follow a marked path. Do not descend towards Santa Marina but stay on a high-level path, which traverses the green hillside below the peaks on the right. This path descends gradually to take you all the way to Posada. There are many cattle tracks, so the main path can be hard to follow, but some landmarks to help you are these: follow some small concrete posts, which mark a municipal boundary; halfway back to Posada, keep to the right above a prominent rocky outcrop; pass a *fuente* (if you can find it); and eventually descend the open hillside to skirt to the right of woods above Posada. You can see the woods from way up the hill, so they make a good target.

GPS REFERENCES (UTM)

Start point at Pandetrave	347294 4774388
Turn-off for Fuente Dé	348714 4776664
Collado de Remoña (Point A)	349018 4777812
Point B junction	349248 4778168
Pedabejo gully	349620 4778413
Scramble route	349421 4778370

Alto de la Canal	349529 4778743
Cabin in the Vega	349608 4779339
Start ascent	350512 4779169
Peña Remoña summit	351043 4778750
Option Two high-level path	347915 4778075
Option Two further along	347164 4778360

Western massif from Valdeon – **WALK 23**

WALK NO. 26 - CARES GORGE

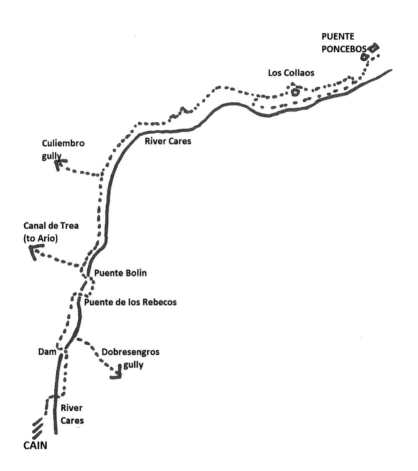

WALK NO. 26 - VARIATION

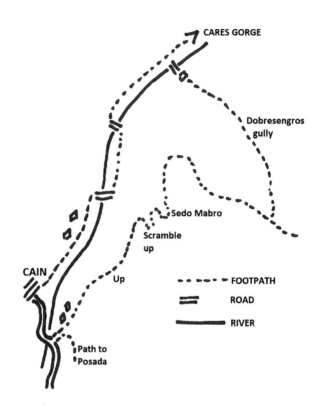

CARES GORGE

Dobresengros gully

Sedo Mabro

Scramble up

CAIN

Up

Path to Posada

- - - - - ► FOOTPATH

ROAD

RIVER

WALK NO. 26

CAIN TO PONCEBOS
THROUGH THE CARES GORGE

This is an easy walk through a spectacular gorge. It is possibly the most popular walk in Spain, and on a trip to the Picos it is really a must. The Cares Gorge, known locally as the Divine Gorge, is without doubt the most emblematic walk of the Picos de Europa.

Distance	22-km return trip
Ascent	400 metres
Overall grade	Easy
Terrain	Good path
Exposure	Lots, but there is ample room to avoid the edge.
Highest point	542 metres

There is a big drop to one side of the path, which may unnerve those with severe vertigo, but the path is two metres wide, giving ample opportunity to stay away from the edge.

At the end of this walk description, I also give details of an excellent variation for the more adventurous, who will need some stamina and a reasonable head for heights.

This walk is 11 km one way (a 22-km round trip). The ascent is 400 metres, and the overall grade is easy. (The additional option is more strenuous).

Cain is a village at the end of the road leading north from Posada de Valdeón. The drive to Cain is spectacular, with the final approach to the village being through a narrow gorge. The walk begins at this isolated village, and follows the course of a hydroelectric canal. A path, built for the construction of the canal, is cut into the cliff faces. Consequently there are often sheer drops of 100 to 200 metres to the side of the 2-metre-wide path, which is unfenced. The gorge is crossed on two bridges.

- From Cain, follow the left bank of the River Cares, and after leaving the last houses cross the river on a footbridge. Follow the right bank, which very soon leads to a dam with a trout ladder alongside the waterfall. This is the beginning of the gorge proper, and of the canal carrying water to a turbine at Puente Poncebos. Cross the dam and follow the path, which leads you safely above the river through tunnels, with fences where you emerge into daylight. Torches are not necessary, but take care that you do not bang your head in the tunnels.

- After leaving the tunnels, simply follow the path. You will soon see the immense gully of Dobresengros ascending on your right, but stay on the left bank, following the main path. You will cross two bridges, firstly the Puente de los Rebecos, and secondly the Puente Bolin. The narrowest stretch of path is on the right bank, between the two bridges. Even so, there is sufficient width to avoid having to walk on the very edge of the drop. Beyond Puente Bolin, the path keeps to the left bank. There is no need to give directions. The only deviations from the main path are those that ascend massive gullies to either side of the gorge. They are of a minimum ascent of about 1,300 metres, so if you go wrong you will soon realise it. Just follow the main path alongside and above the river.

- Two thirds of the way into the walk, beyond the Culiembro gully, you will reach a stone building that is used as a bar at peak times. (They keep the beer in crates in the canal to keep it cool.) Shortly afterwards you will pass a path going down to the right into the gorge. This is an alternative route, but it is often closed due to landslides and I suggest you ignore it.

- The main path ascends a little just beyond here to reach Los Collaos, the highest point of the walk, and it then descends to pass some ruined buildings. Somewhat further on it reaches a dirt track, where you turn left to reach two hotels and bars at Puente Poncebos.

- To return to Cain just walk back the way you came. You can take transport, but a taxi is expensive, because although it is an 11-kilometre walk, it is about 120 kilometres to drive round the perimeter of the mountains.

The walk should take you about three hours in each direction. Since Puente Poncebos is 200 metres lower than Cain, the return leg involves more ascent than the outward leg.

ALTERNATIVE OPTION: SEDO MABRO

If you would like more adventure, and if you have some stamina and a reasonable head for heights, you may choose this option for the start of the walk. This variation adds about 2 km in distance and involves an extra 300 metres of ascent and descent.

From the village of Cain, walk back along the road towards Posada de Valdeón for a couple of hundred metres. Where the road crosses a bridge and swings to the right, take a track to the left. Almost immediately you will see a footpath to the right signposted to Posada, but ignore it and follow the path straight on, with Cain to your left. Go past some farm buildings, and start to ascend gradually, almost parallel to the river. The path is little used but is in good condition (September 2016).

- As the path approaches an apparently impassable cliff, it takes a sharp right turn and ascends through a cleft in the cliff in zigzags. It would classify as a Grade 1 scramble. The ascent is not difficult, but it may not be suitable for anybody unaccustomed to heights. Although there are no major precipices to cross, it has an airy aspect. For scramblers it is an excellent route.

- This path is known as the Sedo de Mabro. A *sedo* is an old drovers' road. Nowadays it is hard to imagine people earning their living by driving goats and sheep over paths such as this, but until the gorge path was built, that is exactly what they did.

- At the top of the *sedo*, you will emerge on to a viewpoint where the village of Cain is below and behind you, with the wide gully of Dobresengros ahead. A good path takes you to the right, alongside the Dobresengros, but keeps to the higher ground above the gully. Soon the path begins to descend gradually. Although the main path continues up the gully, shortly before you reach some major rocks – which dominate the lower part of the valley – a path descends to the left and takes you down to the valley bottom.

- Turn left to follow the stream (dry in summer) downhill, to reach a hut at the bottom of the gully. Cross a wooden bridge over the River Cares and join the main gorge path, where you can turn right to see the rest of the gorge towards Poncebos or turn left to return quickly to Cain.

GPS REFERENCES (UTM)

Start point in Cain	345278 4786285
Bottom of Dobresengros gully	345650 4786714
Bottom of Canal de Trea	346021 4787671
Bottom of Culiembro gully	346544 4789485

Puente Poncebos	351263 4791006
Alternative path	345423 4786026
Sedo de Mabro	345834 4786585
In the Dobresengros gully	346448 4786181

Posada de Valdeon – **WALK 21**

WALK NO. 27 - CAIN TO ARIO VIA THE SEDOS DE OLISEDA

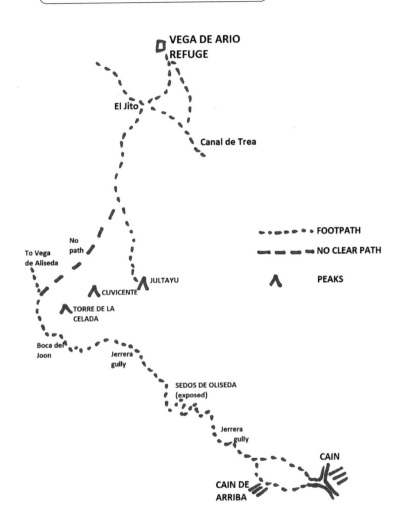

VEGA DE ARIO REFUGE

El Jito

Canal de Trea

FOOTPATH

NO CLEAR PATH

PEAKS

No path

To Vega de Aliseda

JULTAYU

CUVICENTE

TORRE DE LA CELADA

Boca del Joon

Jerrera gully

SEDOS DE OLISEDA (exposed)

Jerrera gully

CAIN

CAIN DE ARRIBA

WALK NO. 27

CAIN TO THE ARIO REFUGE VIA THE SEDOS DE OLISEDA

A steep and long ascent of an enormous gully to a mountain refuge, from where the ascent of several nearby peaks becomes possible. The gully involves a short but exposed scramble. Some off-piste navigation is required in the second section of the walk.

Distance	10 km
Ascent	1,500 metres
Overall grade	Strenuous
Terrain	Footpaths, rocks and grass
Exposure	Considerable
Highest point	1,888 metres

Cain is a remote village at the end of the road into the valley from Posada de Valdeón. It is at the beginning of the Cares Gorge. But this walk does not go into the gorge. Instead, it ascends a massive gully (the Canal de Jerrera) to the north-west, to reach a height close to 2,000 metres.

Even more remote than Cain is the smaller village of Cain de Arriba (Higher Cain). The walk sets off from Cain in the direction of Cain de Arriba, although it is not necessary to actually reach the second village. The path goes to its right-hand (north) side, keeping close to a stream.

- On entering Cain, where the road turns right to follow the river, take the street straight ahead to the left side of the restaurant Casa Cuevas, pass a *fuente* on the left, and go uphill. There is a left turn, which will lead you to Cain de Arriba, but ignore that turn and go straight on to ascend a track. You will soon reach a stream where a path goes left into the smaller village. But at this point cross to the right-hand side of the stream and take a path up to the right. It leads very soon to another stream (the Jerrera), and the route now follows this stream up the gully.

- On reaching the stream, immediately cross it, and take a path on the right-hand side of the stream as you ascend. It zigzags up. Continue up the main gully, ignoring any turn-offs, until you reach an open area where the path goes across to the left and there is a large cairn. Turn right at the cairn. You will ascend towards the Jerrera gully once more, and the path leads you up a grassy hillside to reach a point where the scramble begins.

- It is not the most difficult of scrambles. There is only one awkward step, where you have to get round a prominent rock. But there is a significant drop below, so take care. This is known as the Sedos de Oliseda. It is an old shepherds' route. (Imagine doing this for a living every day.)

- The scramble goes firstly to the right. Then there is a level stretch going left, and the longest part of the scramble commences. The total distance is about 50 metres. You will be across it within a few minutes, and then the path continues with the Jerrera way below you on the left, at the bottom of the now very deep gully. The path is a good one, but there is a drop to the side so take care. As you walk along you can see the remaining part of the gully above, and it is simply a matter of following the path up it.

As you near the top, the path becomes indistinct and you may lose it altogether. It does not really matter as long as you keep going up. But the path 'officially' keeps to the left side of the gully as it nears the top, where you will reach the col at Boca del Joon, with the Joon de Oliseda (a circular valley) beyond. This valley is surrounded by peaks, notably to the left Peña Blanca and Robliza, ahead La Verdillengua, and on your right the three peaks of Torre de la Celada (1,994 metres), Cuvicente (2,014 metres) and Jultayu (1,940 metres).

If you have time, you can ascend any of the three latter summits on your way to the refuge, but that would be additional to the statistics summarised above. It is very easy to reach the little top of la Celada, where a great view awaits you.

The following route will take you to the refuge at the Vega de Ario, where you can stay for a night or two if you wish, and the next day any of those nearby peaks are within reach. (Some of them are very difficult, others less so.)

- From Boca del Joon, the refuge is still over 2 km away in a straight line. You should follow the path to the north-east, and soon you will most likely lose the path and have to make your way across country off-piste. You will need to navigate by compass and intuition. The main thing is to continue in a generally north-westerly direction until you have passed the mountain of Cuvicente. When you are below Jultayu go more or less due north. If you are lucky you may find a footpath here. There are lots of valleys and hills, in a fairly chaotic landscape.

- Do not be tempted to descend in to the huge gully of Canal de Trea, which goes down to the right before the refuge. In other words, do not lose a lot of height. Skirt round to the left of any large sinkholes you encounter en route. If the weather is clear (and I would certainly not recommend this route in mist) you should see cabins in the distance to the north, which indicate the whereabouts of the refuge. Before you reach these cabins, aim for a place called El Jitu, where a group of very large cairns indicate that you are at a crossroads of paths. From El Jitu the main path going north of east leads you directly to the Refugio Vega de Ario.

NOTES RE GPS

In the Canal de Jerrera, due to the loss of satellites, GPS tracking is impossible. On the latter section of the walk from Boca del Joon to the refuge you should navigate with map and compass, and if you have GPS all the better.

GPS REFERENCES (UTM)

Start point in Cain	345278 4786285
Canal de la Jerrera	344709 4786459
The Sedos de Oliseda (exposed)	343965 4786801
Top of Jerrera (Boca del Joon)	342893 4787416
Route towards Ario	342941 4787706
El Jito junction	343664 4789158
Ario refuge	343849 4789599
Nearby peaks: Jultayu Cuvicente Torre de la Celada	344119 4787841 343316 4787705 343096 4787561

WALK NO. 28 - ARIO TO CAIN VIA CULLIEMBRO

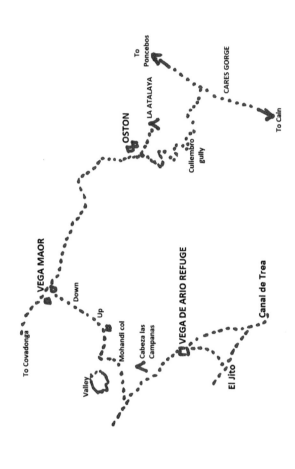

WALK NO. 28

VEGA DE ARIO TO CAIN
VIA THE CULIEMBRO GULLY

The shortest descent to Cain from Ario is via the Canal de Trea, which goes steeply down directly from the refuge to the Cares Gorge. But instead of making an immediate descent, this route stays high, crosses open land to descend gradually to the meadows of Vega de Maor, visits a viewpoint over the Cares at Oston, and descends the Culiembro gully to reach the gorge, and then on to Cain.

Distance	14 km
Ascent	275 metres (1,400 metres descent)
Overall grade	Moderate
Terrain	Footpaths, rocks and grass. Navigation skills required.
Exposure	None, apart from the Cares Gorge (see Walk 26).
Highest point	1,665 metres

The early stages of this walk are on vague or non-existent paths, so *you will need a good map and compass to navigate the route.*

- On exiting the door of the refuge at Vega de Ario, turn left. At the crest of a hill, look for a path going north-west. It leads into a valley, and continues north-west and downhill. Keep straight on downhill, to the western side of the hill of Cabeza las Campanas.

- About a kilometre from the refuge and at roughly 1,500 metres altitude, turn to the right and traverse to the east, with a valley below to your left. At the far side of the traverse you will reach the col of Mohandi. Cross to the far side of the col and descend to another valley with a cabin, from where you should go to the north to cross the col of Les Cuerries, and then descend over rocky ground to the north-east to reach the meadows and cabins at Vega Maor.

• Here you will meet the main west to east path, which links the Covadonga lakes to the northern end of the Cares Gorge. It is part of la Ruta de la Reconquista (the Reconquest Route), which relates to the history and the legends of the area.

• At Vega Maor turn right. The path goes easily across meadowland slightly south of east, until after a steeper descent some 3 km from Vega Maor it reaches the *majada* (herders' huts) of Oston. Pause here to visit the viewpoint of La Atalaya, which is the hill straight ahead as you arrive at Oston. It is easy enough to ascend. It is a spectacular balcony high above the gorge.

• Return from La Atalaya to the Oston cabins and go left (south), down into the big gully of Culiembro. The path is well defined, if rather stony at times. It zigzags continually down, passing below an enormous cave (used as a goat shelter) and continues, passing a *fuente* lower down, to reach the footpath through the Cares Gorge, where you are likely to meet lots of other walkers. For Cain turn right along the gorge path and follow it all the way. (For Poncebos turn left instead.)

GPS REFERENCES (UTM)

Start point at Ario	343849 4789599
Mohandi col	343448 4790361
Vega Maor	344377 4791256
Oston	345935 4790151
Cares Gorge at base of Culiembro	346550 4789506

WALK NO. 29 - PANDERRUEDAS TO JARIO

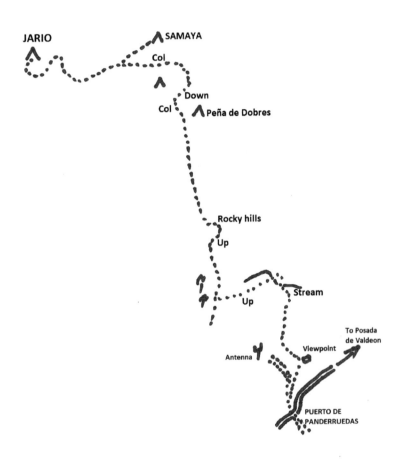

JARIO

SAMAYA

Col

Down

Col

Peña de Dobres

Rocky hills

Up

Up

Stream

To Posada
de Valdeon

Antenna

Viewpoint

PUERTO DE
PANDERRUEDAS

WALK NO. 29

PANDERRUEDAS TO THE PEAK OF JARIO

An easy to moderate walk, depending on which options you take. The route goes to some of the peripheral peaks to the south-west of the Western massif, with brilliant views into the higher mountains.

Distance	12 km
Ascent	600 metres
Overall grade	Easy to moderate
Terrain	Footpaths, rocks and grass
Exposure	None, but a slightly airy final ascent.
Highest point	1,922 metres

An extension to the walk allows you to walk back to Posada de Valdeón, an extra 6 km distance and an extra 600 metres of descent, through pasture and woods. This would make the overall grade for the walk strenuous.

On the road from Posada de Valdeón to the west, there is a viewpoint at Puerto de Panderruedas, with a parking area and picnic benches. Start here, on the right-hand side of the road coming from Posada.

- Go north through a gate in the fence, cross a meadow and then take a track going uphill. The track keeps to the right of, and below, a hill with a transmitter on top. At a track junction, keep right. You will soon reach a monstrous concrete structure that was built as a viewpoint. It is an ugly thing, but the view is great. (*When I took a mountaineering friend there for his first view of the Picos he said he must have died and gone to heaven.*)

- Go down a couple of steps at the far side of the viewpoint to pick up the path to the right. It leads through beech and oak woods, crosses a stream and follows the stream (which is on your left) uphill for a short way to reach open meadows. At this point, do not go straight on, but turn left, cross the stream again, and follow a path uphill. After walking through heather on a good path, you will reach another open area with trees on the far side. You may be tempted to turn left here, but our route goes steeply up to the right on a green strip of land alongside the trees.

- At the top of the rise, turn right and continue on the path – which soon goes uphill once more, to reach a hillside with some interesting conglomerate rock. As you reach the rocks the path takes a sharp left turn, which you may not see at once. Go to the left on the path, which soon levels out. The path skirts the western flank of the Peña de Dobres, going down a little and then up again, and then reaches a pass, the Dobres col (*shown on the Adrados map as Cdnas. De Dobres*).

From the col, follow the path down to the right for a short distance, and then ascend to the left on steep grassy slopes between two hills. The top of the slope is Collada Blanca. The hill immediately on the left is Peña Blanca (the White Hill), and the hill on the right, of brown rock, is Samaya. At 1,805 metres altitude, Peña Blanca is easily accessible by turning left at the top of the slope and just walking up the incline.

- For the peak of Jario, continue beyond Peña Blanca on a path going slightly to the right, and make for a col to the left of the peak of Samaya (which you can ascend on the return leg). At this col, turn left along a vague path over and round a hilltop, and then a clear path leads you in a westerly direction towards the peak of Jario (1,913 metres). The path ascends a broad green slope to the eastern side of the summit and then crosses a grassy platform, from where a right turn leads to the final summit. Although this hill is peripheral to the central peaks, it is a fine peak in its own right, and in fact the final ascent may be just a little daunting for those with vertigo.

- From Jario, return the way you came as far as the col at the base of Samaya. If you wish to ascend Samaya, just follow the ridge up to the summit. You will find bits of path at times, but much of the ascent is scrambling over boulders and through heather. This ascent has become quite difficult and scratchy (at October 2019) due to the overgrown state of the heather. Return by the same route to the col, and turn left to return to Collada Blanca. Descend to the east and then ascend to the right to return to the Dobres col. From there follow the outward path back to Panderruedas.

ALTERNATIVE:

If you wish to walk back to Posada de Valdeón, descend the green valley to the north-east from the base of Samaya and follow a path by a stream. After 400 metres turn right, where a wooden signpost shows the way, and continue over mainly open ground. You will descend a little to cross a stream. And then, after ascending slightly, you will reach the Puerto de Dobres, a green pass. Here the path goes steeply downhill and slightly to the right.

- Follow the path down (south and then very soon east), and into woods. Continue (seemingly interminably) on the path until it joins a dirt road, and follow the dirt road down to the right. It will bring you eventually to the village of Caldevilla, and you can keep straight on the track for Posada. This leg turns an easy day into a strenuous one.

GPS REFERENCES (UTM)

Start point at Panderruedas	338822 4776603
Viewpoint	338887 4777051

Turn left	338759 4777672
Turn right	338244 4777569
Collada Blanca	338094 4779386
Pico Samaya	337888 4779535
Route to Jario	337371 4779323
Pico Jario summit	337016 4779400
Puerto de Dobres	338666 4779729
Path down	339565 4779552

The Lago de Ercina – **WALK 32**

WALK NO. 30 - PANDERRUEDAS TO GILDAR

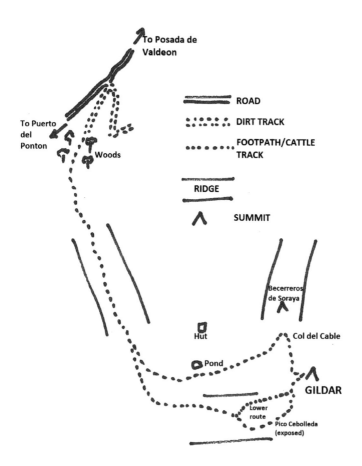

WALK NO. 30

PANDERRUEDAS TO THE PEAK OF GILDAR
(2,078 metres)

Distance	14 km
Ascent	890 metres
Overall grade	Moderate
Terrain	Footpaths, rocks and grass
Exposure	None, but with an optional exposed scramble.
Highest point	2,078 metres

Navigation can be difficult in mist, in which case return by the way you came.

Drive from Posada de Valdeón past Soto de Valdeón and Caldevilla, and continue up the hill for about 10 km to reach the large car park and viewpoint at Panderruedas (not the smaller viewpoint on a bend halfway up the hill). Park at Panderruedas.

The peak of Gildar is at an altitude of over 2,000 metres. But it is on the perimeter of the Picos and is relatively easy to reach, compared to some of the more central mountains. It is situated to the south-east side of Panderruedas.

* On arriving from Posada, take a track to the left (south) from the car park. The track separates into two almost immediately after leaving the road. Take the right fork and continue through the deciduous woods. At a junction keep left. The track crosses a clearing (go straight on) and ascends through woods. It emerges onto a broad ridge, with grassy and shaly terrain. Keep to the high point of the ridge as best you can.

- There are cattle tracks all over the place, which look like good footpaths. Generally speaking, just keep to the high ground. You will ascend gradually. As you near the higher parts of the ridge (at about GPS 339393 4773507), you have a choice. Continuing on the ridge will lead you to a very narrow section, Pico Cebolleda, shortly before the ascent to the main peak of Gildar. ***Be warned: this ridge is a sharp edge and involves an easy but exposed scramble.*** The easier option from the above GPS mark, or from anywhere on the lower part of the ridge, is to take any of several cattle tracks to the left, crossing the head of the valley below the ridge, to make a direct approach towards Gildar itself.

- If you do the scramble over Pico Cebolleda, at the far end simply continue up to the summit of Gildar.

- If the weather is clear you will have a good view of the options. The tracks are animal trails, not footpaths, but there are plenty of them and they make for good walking.

The peak of Gildar is some 2 km as the crow flies from the GPS point above. Once you are on the eastern side of the valley, the ascent to the peak is just an uphill walk. From the summit of Gildar there are great views of the main massifs of the Picos and of the Valdeón valley.

- From the summit, follow the crest of the hill to the north over boulders and scrub to the Horcada del Cable col, and then make your way downhill to the west into the valley below. There are no formal paths but, again, lots of cattle tracks. Continue downhill to reach a delightful small lake, which makes a great place for a rest. Then continue to the west, ascend easily to join the ridge you ascended early in the walk, turn right at the top and follow the path back through the woods to Panderruedas.

GPS REFERENCES (UTM)

Start point at Panderruedas	338822 4776603
Through the woods	338429 4775620
On the ridge	339393 4773507
Pico Cebolleda (exposed)	340747 4772888
Gildar summit	341265 4773534
Horcada del Cable	340997 4773925

La Junciana – **WALK 9**

WALK NO. 31 - TORRE DEL FRIERO

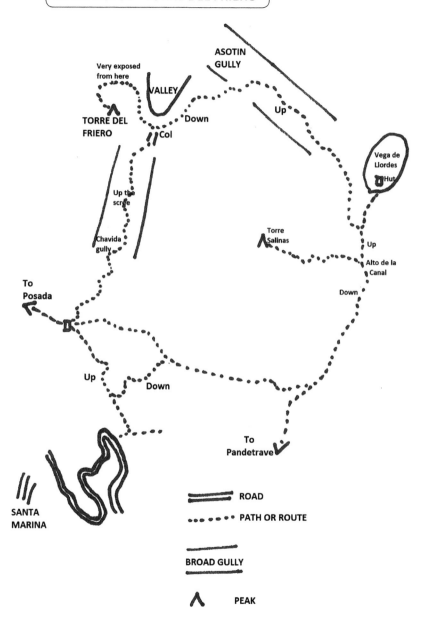

ASOTIN GULLY

Very exposed from here

VALLEY

Down

TORRE DEL FRIERO

Col

Up

Vega de Llordes

Hut

Up the scree

Torre Salinas

Up

Chavida gully

Alto de la Canal

To Posada

Down

Up

Down

To Pandetrave

SANTA MARINA

━━━━ ROAD

••••••• PATH OR ROUTE

━━━ BROAD GULLY

⋀ PEAK

WALK NO. 31

TORRE DEL FRIERO
AND THE CANAL DE ASOTIN

A circular walk to the exposed peak of Torre del Friero, and circuiting through the higher parts of the Canal de Asotin to return more easily to the start of the walk. *This route would be dangerous in mist.*

Distance	16 km
Ascent	1,360 metres
Overall grade	Strenuous
Terrain	Massive scree ascent, rock scramble and footpaths
Exposure	Severe exposure near the summit
Highest point	2,448 metres

From Posada de Valdeón drive south-east towards Puerto de Pandetrave and pass above the village of Santa Marina. Beyond that village, go round some sharp bends. Shortly there is a very pronounced left-hand bend, followed by an equally pronounced right-hand bend. Just beyond these two bends, as the road takes a straighter line, park on the right-hand side of the road, near a footpath to the left signposted for Fuente Dé.

• At the start of the walk, do not follow the signpost. Instead navigate to the north-west. There is no defined footpath, but most of the ground is grassy and open. However, there are patches of scrub, which you will need to either circumnavigate, or alternatively bushwhack your way through. As you ascend to the north-west, aim towards the massive scree-filled gully Canal de la Chavida – which, assuming the weather is clear, you can hardly mistake. (Torre del Friero is the apparently inaccessible peak above the left side of the gully.)

- You will soon cross a minor, grassy valley, and then continue towards the big gully. Below the base of the gully you will find a hut, the Chozo de Urdias.

- From the hut, walk up into the gully by whichever route you find easiest. It becomes a massive scree. There are cairns scattered around, but there is no definitive route. *(I have been informed in October 2019 that there is now a clear path up the scree, but since it is some months since I made the ascent I can not guarantee this.)* For me, the easiest route to the top is close the left-hand edge of the scree. However, at the very top you need to pass through the col (the Horcada de Chavida), which is closer to the right-hand side. So you must either struggle up the right side of the gully or cross it near the top.

- The route descends on the far side of the *horcada.* Keep to the left, very close to the eastern base of Torre del Friero. At the bottom of a descent, a path leads you round the base of the mountain, and ascends to the left on its northern side. This section of the walk, while impressive, is easy. But it soon changes. At the top of an incline, a rocky platform gives you your first startling view down to the west. The path now goes left, hugging tight to the mountainside, and now begins the more difficult section.

- You will encounter a rounded, smooth rock, with a sort of cavity on the right-hand side, above a deep slope. ***If you ascend this rock, keeping left, remember that you will have to come back the same way. If you find that a daunting prospect, do not ascend it.***

Scramble up the said rock to reach a platform with an absolutely brilliant view down on to pinnacles leading down to Valdeón. Continue across the platform. Then comes the second tricky move, where you must stride round a rock while holding on with both hands. It is a single step, but there is a severe, perpendicular drop below. ***Again, remember that you will be returning the same way.*** Once across this rock, there remains a rocky ascent of slightly over 100 metres to reach the summit. It is rock all the way and not for vertigo sufferers. There is an easy scramble up a gully, followed by a more difficult second scramble. Some red paint marks help to show the way. None of this is easy, and remember that you will have to come back down it.

Return carefully. It is essential that you find the same route. Descend the scramble sections and then follow the outward route all the way back to the Horcada de Chavida.

• For a direct return to your car, descend the scree slope to the south and back to the start.

For the full circuit, descend from Horcada de Chavida to the north, but keep close to the eastern (right) side above a deep valley. You should soon find a footpath that descends over rocky ground. The path quickly swings more to the east, and leads you to the higher reaches of the Canal de Asotin (the major gully connecting Valdeón to the Vega de Llordes above). Although you will be descending towards the Asotin, do not be in a hurry to descend directly, as the Asotin rises to meet you, and in fact this footpath leads you uphill at times. If you lose the path, use your intuition and your compass to go south-east and then south. Eventually you will meet the path, which ascends from the Vega de Llordes to a high point at Alto de la Canal. Turn right on the path to reach the top.

• From this rocky promontory, follow the path to the south into a small valley. But, before descending the large gully, leave the valley by a cairn on a path going south-west and rising slightly. It quickly reaches a level area with cairns, and then begins a descent. The path is good at first, but becomes a scramble down a rocky face. The scrambling is easy, but care must be taken. At the foot of the scramble, the path leads you above the Fuente de Pedabejo (where there is cool water). Go to the right above the *fuente*, across pastures, and follow the marked path on to a broader track, which leads you to an open grassy area where several paths cross and cars may be parked. This area is known as Caben de Remoña.

At this point, take a path down into a short narrow gully, cross a stream, and follow the marked path (which leads all the way to Posada de Valdeón). The path leads you to the Chozo de Urdias (the hut you visited early in the walk), but you can take a shortcut at an earlier point and make your way down the open hillside to reach the bend in the road where the walk began. You should see the bend in the road from much higher up the hill.

GPS REFERENCES (UTM)

Start point above Santa Marina	347462 4777434
Urdias hut	347278 4778195
Into the Chavida gully	347251 4778921
Horcado de Chavida	347769 4779671
Base of Friero	347701 4779986
Circuiting (exposed)	347553 4780145
Torre del Friero summit	347504 4779985

Longer descent route:	
Descent towards the Asotin	348178 4779946
In the Asotin gully	348671 4780015
Continuing the circuit	349094 4779838
Alto de la Canal	349522 4778761

WALK NO. 32 - LAGO ERCINA TO CAIN VIA ARIO

CAR PARK

Hut

Lake

Up

Fuente

Las Bobias

Up

El Toleyu (huts)

ARIO REFUGE

El Jito

Vega de Aliseda

JULTAYU

Canal de Trea

Puente Bolin

TO CAIN

WALK 32

LAGO DE LA ERCINA TO CAIN
VIA THE ARIO REFUGE

A linear walk from the beautiful Lake Ercina on a well-marked footpath to a remote mountain refuge, followed by a big descent to the Cares Gorge and through it to the village of Cain.

Distance	17 km
Ascent	750 metres
Overall grade	Strenuous
Terrain	Good footpaths, with a long, steep descent.
Exposure	Nil, apart from in the Cares Gorge (see Walk 26).
Highest point	1,650 metres

Since it is a linear walk you will need to have transport or accommodation at Cain. With accommodation you could return via Walk 27 on the following day. Other alternatives are below:

(i) Go as far as the refuge and then retrace your steps.

(ii) Ascend the peak of Jultayu (elevation 1,942 metres),

From Cangas de Onis drive to Covadonga and continue up a steep and bendy road to reach the second of two lakes, Lago de la Ercina. (Take care on the road, which is in good condition but is narrow at times.) At the lake there is a large car park and a bar/restaurant. Park there, or take the bus from Covadonga. In the summer months you may be obliged to take the bus, as the road can be closed to other traffic.

- From the car park by the lake, walk along the left-hand side of the lake. The path soon ascends to the left and passes by a hut near rocks. It is a well-marked path, leading up a grassy hillside on a route that can be very muddy. It levels out at the top, and soon the high peaks of the Central massif appear ahead. (The mountain with a flattish top is Torre Cerredo, the high point of the Picos.)

- Continue on this path over undulating and generally easy ground, and on a very slight descent you will reach the Majada de las Bobias (a group of farm huts). Just beyond the *majada* is a rocky area with a *fuente* (a water source), which can be very refreshing in hot weather. (Whether you wish to drink hill water is up to you, of course.) At the *fuente* a path goes down to the left, but our path goes up to the right. Go across to the right and uphill to get above the trees. From here the path goes gradually uphill, with a view down to the huts of La Redondiella below on the left. Soon you will reach a valley with a pond (which may be dry in late summer), and the path now climbs on the left side in zigzags. Continue uphill, keeping to higher ground. The route is fairly well marked with paint. It will lead you, 6 km from the start of the walk, to a group of large cairns, marked on the maps of the area and called El Jitu.

- The path levels out and then swings gradually to the left to lead you to the Vega de Ario and its mountain refuge. There are refreshments here, and also a *fuente* for fresh water, although in dry seasons it can reduce to a trickle. (Recently there were no toilets. They were said to be under repair.)

- To continue the route to Cain you should descend to the Cares Gorge via the Canal de Trea. This involves a descent of some 1,200 metres, all of it on a good footpath. In order to find it, leave the refuge and cross the Vega de Ario (the meadows surrounding the refuge) in a southerly direction, heading towards Jultayu, which is the nearest of the peaks to your right. About 650 metres from the refuge you will reach the col of Las Cruces, where you will find a path descending to the south-east and entering into the great void of the Trea gully. Although the size of the gully may be daunting this is a popular route, and the path is in good condition. It zigzags its way downhill, and despite the airy position it does not reach the edge of any precipices, and involves no significant exposure. However, take great care on the descent not to lose the path, as any alternative would be dangerous.

- There is possible confusion at one point where the path stays high and goes to the left of a deep gully. If you lose the path go back to find it. Other than that, simply follow the path all the way until you pass through woods and arrive at the broad, stony track alongside the canal in the Cares Gorge. Turn right along it and you will reach Cain within a distance of about 2 kilometres.

OPTION Jultayu peak

- From the Ario refuge, cross the vega to the south, and at the point where the path descends into the Canal de Trea, stay high instead, and take a good path to the right of the Trea, which ascends directly to the skyline and the peak of El Jultayu. The ascent is not difficult. It is simply a walk. But when you arrive at the summit it will take your breath away. The village of Cain is 1,500 metres below and you can see straight down.

- At the summit, turn right to follow the edge of the ridge as closely as you can, and pick up a route (you may find an intermittent path) to the right, which leads you downhill over rough ground to the cairns at El Jitu, from where the path to the north-west leads you back to the Lago de la Ercina.

157

GPS REFERENCES (UTM)

Start point at Lago de la Ercina	339205 4792921
Las Bobias	340961 4791315
Ascending	342689 4789947
El Jito	343664 4789158
Ario refuge	343849 4789599
Col of Las Cruces	344069 4788639
Cares Gorge at Puente Rebecos	345964 4787513
Jultayu peak	344119 4787841

Pico Padierna from Vega de Llordes – **WALK 18**

WALK NO. 33 - LA REDONDIELLA

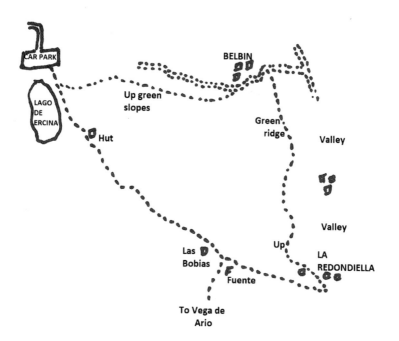

WALK NO. 33

LA REDONDIELLA CIRCUIT FROM LAGO DE LA ERCINA

An easy, circular walk from the beautiful Lake Ercina.

Distance	8 km
Ascent	350 metres
Overall grade	Easy
Terrain	Good footpaths
Exposure	None
Highest point	1,300 metres

The first part of this walk covers the same ground as the first part of Walk 32, but this route provides an easy circuit through lovely scenery and with views to the high mountains.

From Cangas de Onis follow the driving instructions in Walk 32 and park near the lake.

- From the car park, walk along the left-hand side of the lake. The path starts to ascend to the left, and passes a hut near some rocks. It is a well-marked path, leading up a grassy hillside on a route that can be very muddy. It levels out at the top, and soon the high peaks of the Central massif appear ahead.

- Continue on this path over undulating and generally easy ground, and on a very slight descent you will reach the Majada de las Bobias (a group of farm huts). Just beyond the *majada* is a rocky area with a *fuente* (a water source). From the *fuente*, while the marked path to Ario goes up to the right, for this route take another path going down to the left.

- The path descends diagonally through beech woods, crossing some stony and maybe muddy ground, to quickly reach the lovely meadows surrounding the ruined huts of La Redondiella. This is a delightful spot, and judging from the number of ruined cabins here, it must have been a hive of activity in times past. Nowadays it is normally deserted, even by hikers, as it is not on any established route.

- At La Redondiella, turn left and walk downhill at first, but keep the watercourse in the valley bottom to your right. Do not follow the valley bottom, but instead keep left and look for a path that starts a little distance from the ruins and goes in a north-westerly direction. The path ascends gradually, as the watercourse descends, and very soon the valley bottom will be way below on your right. Keep to the path and now go almost north, until you find yourself walking along a lovely green ridge with cabins in a meadow way below on the right. Approximately 2 km from La Redondiella, at the far end of the ridge, you will find a dirt track, which descends to the left to the *majada* (the meadow and the cabins) of Belbin.

- The Belbin cabins, unlike at La Redondiella, are still in use as cattle winterings, and you may find herders here. One of the cabins has solar panels. Go down to Belbin. Beyond the cabins a dirt track leads all the way back to Lago de la Ercina. However, you need not follow the track itself. The green pastures make for very good and easy walking, so keep well to the left of the track on grass. As the land rises, you will see a hilltop to the left. Do not ascend it. Stay on the slopes to its right, until you reach a crest with a great view of the lake. An easy descent across open ground then leads back to the car park.

- To the right of the car park you can make an interesting diversion to walk through a disused mining area and down to a visitor centre, beyond which you will also find the bus stop for Covadonga.

GPS REFERENCES (UTM)

Start point at Lago de la Ercina	339205 4792921
Las Bobias	340961 4791315
La Redondiella	341528 4791189
Ridge	341187 4792237
Belbin	340827 4792733

WALK NO. 34 - MIRADOR DE ORDIALES

WALK NO. 34

MIRADOR DE ORDIALES AND PICO COTALBA

A linear walk to a spectacular viewpoint and also a nearby peak.

Distance	12 km linear
Ascent	1,050 metres
Overall grade	Moderate
Terrain	Footpaths, good tracks and a little scrambling on rock.
Exposure	Nil, but be careful at the viewpoint.
Highest point	2,026 metres

From Cangas de Onis drive to Covadonga and continue up a steep and bendy road to reach the first of two lakes, Lago Enol. As you reach the lake, a minor road goes to the right. Turn into this road and park where you can. (The further along it you can get, the more you will reduce the walking distance.)

At the far end of the walk, return the way you came, or you could spend the night at the Vegarredonda refuge and do further walking from there on the next day.

- From the lake, walk (or drive) south and then south-west along a good dirt road. After 2.5 km, at a junction of tracks at Pan de Carmen, turn left. The track takes a zigzag route, and about 1 km from Pan de Carmen it swings to the right and ascends to the Vega de Piedra (Stony Meadow), where you should turn left and ascend the gradual slope to the south-east.

- The path, which is signposted to Vegarredonda, leads you past some huts at La Rondiella (not to be confused with La Redondiella in Walk 33). Continue past the huts and you will soon arrive at the Vegarredonda refuge.

- From the refuge, continue on the good path going south, but after only 200 metres leave the main path and turn right on another path, which goes west. It takes a few bends, swings south and then west again, and then swings left (south) once more. Continue on the path to pass a hut/refuge (unmanned) and very shortly you will reach the Mirador de Ordiales, where a natural parapet protects you from the edge of the precipice below. You will be looking down into the valley of the Rio Dobra, almost 1,000 metres below. A spectacular place.

- From the mirador, return along the footpath the way you came for about 100 metres or so and turn right to ascend to the peak of Cotalba. You may find an intermittent path, but you can use your intuition and navigate to the peak in a south-easterly direction from the mirador, over a distance of only 1 kilometre. Depending on your exact route, you may find some easy rock scrambling on the way.

- From the peak, return by the outward route to Vegarredonda.

GPS REFERENCES (UTM)

Start point at Lago de Enol	337975 4792653
Pan de Carmen	336859 4791937
Vega de Piedra	336798 4791102
Vegarredonda refuge	338133 4788872
Turn right	338273 4788707
Mirador de Ordiales	336611 4787781
Pico Cotalba	337165 4787503